T0157539

A View from the Street/
River City Policing

A View from the Street/ River City Policing

S. HENRY KNOCKER

A View from the Street/River City Policing

iUniverse books may be ordered through booksellers or by contacting:

iUniverse
1663 Liberty Drive
Bloomington, IN 47403
www.iuniverse.com
1-800-Authors (1-800-288-4677)

Because of the dynamic nature of the Internet, any web addresses or links contained in this book may have changed since publication and may no longer be valid. The views expressed in this work are solely those of the author and do not necessarily reflect the views of the publisher, and the publisher hereby disclaims any responsibility for them.

Any people depicted in stock imagery provided by Thinkstock are models, and such images are being used for illustrative purposes only. Certain stock imagery © Thinkstock.

ISBN: 978-1-4917-6320-9 (sc)
ISBN: 978-1-4917-6319-3 (e)

Library of Congress Control Number: 2015904883

Print information available on the last page.

iUniverse rev. date: 04/14/2015

Preface

I am writing this book to inform the reader in somewhat of a light hearted way as to the making of an average police officer. The book delves into some of what I went through before making my choice to dedicate my life to the cause of policing. My Life as a child, Solider, and a young man coming to grips with learning disabilities that early on affected my job prospects. It encompasses a number of experiences with a variety of social misfits and ordinary folk just trying to extricate themselves from sticky situations. Some are funny and others tragic. I give my opinions as to what makes a good Police officer and police chief and take them both to task in different ways in this book. The book is arranged to give the reader as broad as possible look at several areas of police interactions with criminals and the courts as well as political commentaries. I explore root causes of racial tension and my feeling as to what the basic attitude that the police should take in respect to race in this country.

Table of Contents

Dedication

I dedicate this book to my wife Carol with whom I have spent the best 47 years of my life, without who's support I could never have gotten through the low spots.

Acknowledgments

My Thanks to Mary Mclean and my granddaughter Haley for their help in editing, and pastor John Hagee for his inspiration and support over the past 30 years

Part One:

Judgment vs. Man's law

March 1 2014

Chapter 1

The Police

Shortly after I joined the Police in "River City" I was riding with one of the old veteran officers. We were talking and the conversation was somehow turned to the topic of who were the worst drivers. He postulated that Asians were worst, old people were second, and women were third.

That's when I bit. I asked the question. What do you do when you see an old Asian woman driving in front of you? His answer came quickly. TURN LEFT!

Don't let your personal feelings about people affect your judgment about anything, in this job. I had been set up, but the lesson was clear. I have never forgotten the lesson.

There is a constant drum beat from media types, both on the left and the right, as to the issue of judging others. When an individual, usually form the left but sometimes from the right also, wants to make the point that we should not judge others. They point to the bible and give us the judge not least you be judged speech.

The confusion lies with Sin vs. laws made by man. This calls for a definition of sin.

"What is sin?" Sin is not robbing banks or beating up grandma. Sin is living your life as though the word of God means nothing in your life."

We are therefore called not to judge others in their relationship to God.

We can, and do, make judgments about the conduct of people as it relates to their interactions with others and the laws of man.

If I believe that people getting tattoos is proof that once in their life they did something stupid. I can do that. I am not making a judgment as to their relationship with the God.

If I sit on a jury, I am not making a judgment as to a person's relationship to God. I am judging whether that person has, without justification, transgressed the laws of man. We leave the matter of whether this is sin up to God.

Therefore, the homosexual, atheist, back slider and hypocrite can all sit next to me in church. I want to be there and I want them there. This living up to the word of God thing is hard stuff. Ask a priest.

If we don't attend church, I believe we are cowards, unable or unwilling to look into our soul. If I am uneasy when sitting next to a person with tattoos all over his or her body, it is because nature has taught me to be wary of colorfully marked beast of all types.

Why am I so down on tattoos you may ask? Let me answer this by saying this— after spending 28 years booking idiots into jail, and filling out booking forms, I noticed that under the box marked "marks, scars and tattoos," the more that went in there, the less charming the individual seemed to be.

When I started reading Dr. Seuss books to my kids, I read "The Star Bellied Sneetches." I realized that vanity can be a problem. Tattoos are vain, and are hard to undo. Fads come and go, but stupid goes clear to the bone.

Wisdom is gained slowly with careful deliberation. These truths I have learned.

College professors need to teach, and stay away from politics. They should keep our kids out of politics until they have developed the wisdom to discern truth from political spin. This would also have the effect of reducing unrest on campuses. Politics is a dirty business and there is nothing, in my judgment, that is particularly in lighting about it that should be compatible with higher learning.

All public employees need to be fired for getting involved in politics. The public employees were granted protections and job security because of political cronyism in the spoils area. Public employees should not be involved in or be allowed to make political contributions to politicians. Public employees promotions need to be based on merit not on how politically active they are. Politicians need to be kicked in the butt if they try to corrupt public employees or, stay in office more than two terms.

Mothers and fathers need to be spanked if they don't correct their children, and have complete control of them, by age 2.

Fathers need to be spanked if they don't get down on the floor with the little ones and roll around till mom gets a headache. Then dad needs to tell mom how pretty she is, and they will all live happily ever after. Dad may be the commander but mom is the top sergeant and should be given the respect that comes with running the company.

Finally don't let your personal feelings about people affect your judgment about anything.

Having said this; the reader needs to understand that people join the police for a variety of reasons. Some want a pay check. Some want to serve their community. Some want to right some wrong, and some do it for the trill of it.

I was on a stakeout with one of our senior detectives in River City. We were talking and he asked me why I had joined the force? I told him that I had always wanted to be a police officer and had been a MP in the army. Then I said why did you join? He said for the thrill of it. I was surprised by his answer so I said "the Thrill of It". He said Yah! When he was a rookie on a department in Oregon he was with an old timer. It was a quite fogy night. They had been patrolling down the main street in the town when they noticed a log truck parked on the side of the rode. It had emergency lights on and warning signs set out behind the truck to the rear. They noted this and went on with the mundane tasks of checking buildings. The radio for the most part was quiet. Along about 2 AM the silence was broken by radio traffic from a nearby town. They were in pursuit of a red corvette. The chase went on for about five to ten minutes. Then the old guy's ears perked up. He slammed on the breaks. Turned the patrol car around and headed back to town. He asked what was going on. The old guy didn't say a word; he just raced back down town. He positioned the patrol car on a side street near the logging truck they had passed earlier. What was going on he asked the old guy just said "watch and see" then we could hear the chase coming in on the main road. When the chase got within a half mile of their location the old guy picked up the mic., and said chase units slow down danger ahead. The chase units slowed, but the corvette kept coming it hit the back of the logging truck and exploded in a huge fireball. Car parts rained down all around them. When the explosion was over the old guy turned to his partner and in wide eyed exclamation just said, "SPECTACULAR".

Chapter 2

The Sage

If I am going to put myself out there, as some kind of sage, you need to understand where I come from.

I was born to a middle class family, made poor by the sheer number of us kids it produced, eleven all totaled. Dad was a foreman at the steel mill. My grandmother had ten. Six were still at home. We lived next door to them; in the Little City Farms area, south of the city. Some people called the area Pigeon Point. It was one of the poor sections of the city. There was little political interest in this section, other than to use it to supplant funds from a sewer project meant to clean up the local creek. The north-end folks wanted to build an aqua theater, on a local lake. They had political muscle. The idea was that the aqua theater performance revenue would pay for the creek cleanup. It never made a dime. They built the thing in the most mosquito infested are of the lake.

The major shopping area was a mile south. It was a rough section of town. I got my butt kicked by two different gangs, one white and one black. I was a victim of street gangs by the time I was fourteen. My dad didn't help things out by giving me the nick name of Slugger. I had beaned him with a Coke bottle when I was two, and that was his revenge.

Grade school

1,2,3,4,5,6,7, Highland Park will go to heaven, when they get there they will say, "Cooper go the other way."

In the 1950s, grade school went to the 8th grade. After this you went to high school. I, unfortunately, was in one of the first classes in our school district to be subjected to the junior high system. It is no coincidence that the decline of education in this nation started in the 1950's.

"If you're smart, it doesn't mean you're smart."

Over the years teachers have done an excellent job of promoting themselves. They have made us believe that teaching is this noble profession.

Teachers and others with government jobs sometimes subscribe to an attitude that they should "do the minimum and get the maximum." They do this because it works.

In government, if you do nothing, if you just do enough to get by, you are unlikely to cause controversy within the organization. Initiative is only valued if it makes a politician look good to the public. This is why government fails if it takes over a private sector function. If business gets too cozy with government and is too dependent on government for revenue, the axiom applies there also.

It is only when a strong leader, operating with oversight, and in relative secrecy, with a clear purpose, that government functions reasonably well. This is why the military, FBI, CIA and like agencies generally work well. If they get too politicized, they fail. A case in point is the IRS. This may not apply universally, but in my experience it is true, for the most part.

I have seen one teacher handle a class with 65 students of different ages and abilities. I have seen teachers that can't handle 5 in a class. Class size means nothing.

Evaluation by grade point average is a sorry way to judge a student's abilities. Mastery is the key to evaluation. When you have mastered a subject you should move on. This is imperative for subjects like simple math and reading. Moving a kid up a grade when he or she can't read is foolhardy, and a criminal act in my opinion. Children who master reading can read at a college level by the 4th grade, and sometimes earlier. If your child is not there, double your efforts, find out why.

I insisted that my children read every day. I never cared what they read, as long as it was wholesome reading. My granddaughter once took up the challenge to read a volume of Webster's dictionary. When they love to read they will read anything.

When I was in the second grade, I was sick a lot. I got measles, chickenpox, and mumps and a few others. I had my head slammed into a desk by my second grade teacher because I was having trouble with reading and writing. I was not ready for the third grade. I missed spelling rules and suffered for the rest of my education until I reached college. In college I took a spelling lab and greatly improved my spelling. This spelling lab retaught me the rules. No one had caught the fact that I had missed this part of my education.

The net effect of the way kids are educated in the US school system, is that they are graded down in all their classes if they can't spell and write. This creates insecurity in children. They are afraid to put their ideas on paper. They are criticized and told they are stupid if they can't spell. These sorts of thing cost me a full grade point in high school and college. Had I been in a system where I was graded on mastery, as opposed to being ranked by GPA, and passed along, I believe I would have been far better off.

Too many kids are allowed to graduate as illiterates. Removing the threat of being fired for cause is the reason for the tragedy that is the US education system.

In school, I was a tall quiet kid; easy-going, but there was something about me that caused the so-called tough kids to want to beat me up. The big guys were bad enough; it was the little tough guys that really irritated me.

Somewhere around the 8th grade I got this revelation. They couldn't lose. If I beat them, I was a bully. If they beat me, they were the heroes. I solved the problem by pointing my finger right in the little tough's faces and gave them this warning, "if you beat me, you are a hero, if I beat you I'm a bully. I have no choice. If you persist, win or lose, I will hurt you." They left me alone after that little declaration.

The vice principal in high school was a local college football star; he and I did not get along well. For some reason, I could not walk down the hall without some member of his junior varsity picking a fight. I never understood why. They always got their butts kicked. I learned to box early in life, at the Boys Club. I hated the whole "boys will be boy's thing" that permeated the thinking of adults. Fights were ok, just fight fair. When you don't like to fight, and you are being called out all the time, the whole thing gets tiresome.

In grade school I played their game. Because I boxed, I could dance around and make the fools miss. I would hit them over and over in the same spot, usually the right shoulder. After about five blows, they couldn't lift their arm any more. When I reached junior high, the kids were a lot bigger. They started ganging up, and pushing us new kids around. I took to using feet and fists. The first guy always got my foot to his groin, and a straight right to the jaw. I ended many fights in this manner.

Once in high school, I heard all day that after school, I was going to get my butt kicked by "the Sailor." They were to wait for me by "The Tree" (a spot in the woods on the way home). When I got there, sure enough there was a guy waiting. He announced he was going to "kick my butt."

There were about 15 or 20 on-lookers, several of whom were obviously the ones that recruited the Sailor. After telling the group that I had no wish to fight, I called the Sailor over to me. I knelt down by the tree. I beckoned him down next to me. I whispered to him, "These guys are not worth getting hurt over." Sailor said, "You are not going to get out of it." I looked into his eyes, and then closed my fist over a hand full of dirt I had been stirring on the ground. When we stood up I threw the dirt in his eyes and took him down by the collar to the ground. I smacked him once in the nose. I then asked him if he wanted to continue this fight. He said, "No!" I let him go and walked on. Half the kids there were standing with their mouths open, and the others were yelling, that's not fair! "I'm not going to fight fair," was my response. "Leave me alone!" I never saw the Sailor again.

The threats and intimidation continued until, I was thrown out of high school in my junior year.

In May 1963, the vice principal confronted me in the hall at the high school, by grabbing me as I walked by. He shoved me into the lockers and stared at me. I shoved him back into the lockers across the hall, and that was that; out I went. To this day, I don't know why that man had it in for me. It may have been that I was skipping school a lot. School was boring for me; I had trouble with spelling, a lot of trouble, and some dyslexia. All the classes marked you down for spelling. It was like being a great swimmer, trying to swim up a water fall. I was staying afloat but not getting anywhere.

That spring I got a job on a floating cannery in Alaska. I worked there until the mosquitos ran me out in June. Mosquitos for some reason like the taste of me. The only thing that I have found that keeps them off me is vitamin B complex. I take it every day during mosquito season.

In 1966 while serving in the Army at Ft. Polk, I was attacked so bad, I was put in the hospital with over 100 bites on my back. I swam across the Big Bear River with some friends. When we got out of the water, a swarm hit us. They drove us back across the river. When I got out of the river my back was covered with mosquitos. The guys started slapping them till my back was a bloody mess. They took me to the dispensary at the fort and told them I had been attacked by mosquitos. The medic laughed until he saw the mess. Then I was sent to the hospital.

Chapter 3

The Guard

June 30th, 1963, I first joined the National Guard. I was sent to Fort Ord, California, at the end of August where I took basic training. The first week of September, I got a letter from home stating that I had another brother. There were now eight boys and three girls. I was the oldest, and was the one most likely to have to change diapers. I was glad to be in basic.

I liked Army life and was happy to be away from school and life at home. There were about 300 of us in my training unit, including a platoon of Inuit Eskimos from Alaska. We went through basic training pretty much without any hitches. We did have an incident when one of the Inuit didn't understand the translator. He dropped a grenade, instead of throwing it. It was picked up and thrown by the sergeant. Another guy in the platoon fell out of ranks down a hill during our 20 mile forced march.

We were in our final week of basic training when President Kennedy was shot. We were taken from the parade ground back to the barracks. We were told what just happened. We stood by all the rest of that day, while rumors circulated about us going to Cuba. We were finally just sent home for Christmas.

M-I-C-K-E-Y U-S-A-T-C

In January I reported to Fort Sill, OK, for advanced artillery training. The Battery Commander at the US Army Training Center was a West Point Officer with a short-timer attitude. He was tough, but every day on our 5-mile run, he would run us past the battalion headquarters and treat the Sgt. Major to a chorus of, "<u>M-I-C-K-E-Y, U-S-A-T-C—MICKEY MOUSE!</u>" Then we would march back to the battery area for chow.

A lot of the guys in my barracks were from wealthy families, and they partied a lot. They would run short of money at the end of the month. My buddy and I would save our money and lend to them at a 100% interest rate till payday. The rate was $10 for $5. We both made out pretty well as the barracks lenders. The first sergeant referred to us as his loan sharks. We never took advantage of a guy that couldn't afford the rates. So he looked the other way.

Artillery training is tough. We all put on muscle. I was 230 lbs. by the time it was over. The two biggest guys in the battery were me and a 250 lb. monster from the eastern part of the state. Once we got into the boxing ring at the urging of the platoon. We sparred a bit. I had learned to box some at the Boys Club. I was able to get out of his way for a while, but he caught me with a jab that parted my gloves and sent me clear across the ring. Nobody messed with him. I saw the guy years later at the race track where I moonlighted as a guard. I heard the name over the page and looked him up. He was half the size he was in the Guard.

Ten weeks later, I went home and rejoined my National Guard unit. I made two meetings. At the end of May 1964, the Guard went to summer camp at the Yakima firing range. We were at the firing range about a week when the new guys were introduced to the 155 Howitzer. The 105s that we trained on were considerably lighter than the 155s. Two guys could easily remove a 105 from a tow hitch. The 155 took four, and you better be ready for the extra weight. Four of us got on the trails of a 155, and lifted it off the tow hook. That's when things went bad for me. When the truck pulled out, instead of letting it down easy, three of them let go. I was on the end of the trails. The trails came down on my feet, driving them into the soft sand of the Yakima firing range. I lost the toenails on both my big toes. My right foot has never been the same since. Despite this mishap, I liked the Army life. I decided then to ask for a transfer to the regular Army.

Chapter 4

The Solider

I was a high school dropout and had received my GED in the US Army. I made rank easy in the Army, despite the spelling thing.

I transferred in to the regular Army in June 1964. I talked my uncle and cousin into joining also. My uncle was three months older than me, and my cousin was a year or so younger. We went in under the buddy system. At that time they were crying for guys to enlist, and they would give you a choice of duty stations. We picked Germany, as that was a three year tour, and little chance of being sent to Vietnam. Screw them college boys, we thought. We could get exempt too. Grandma had lost one son in the Marines in WWII, and another wounded in Korea. She didn't want to lose any more in that "damn war of the Kennedys."

Army Lies

We all went off to Fort Ord, California. They went to basic and I went to a holding company.

We called the unit the 101st Combat Gardeners. There were 29 of us there awaiting orders. Our boss was a grumpy old Master Sergeant, whose weight was about 400 lbs. We kept the grass outside the barracks at exactly two inches tall, and pulled any other details the base commander and others wanted. I kept in touch with the guys when they got a pass or could go to the PX.

About their 9th week in basic, my orders come through. I was off to Track and Wheel School at Fort Sill, OK. Back at Fort Sill, I could visit Grandma and Grandpa about 80 miles east. Two weeks later, the guys showed up.

We did our training; I was two weeks ahead of them. I kept them up on what was coming next. We had it made. I graduated and made PFC the same week. All my class was off to their new units. When the guys were graduated, they got orders for Germany. I was still awaiting my orders. I went to the First Sergeant to let him know that the guys and I were on the buddy system. The first Sergeant said, "PFC Knocker do you like your new rank and the money that goes with it?" I said, "YES, Sergeant!" Then he said, "You're Going to Korea on a ship. You get to see the whole damn Pacific."

I thought about going to the Inspector General., but the First Sergeant gave me the best advice you can get in the Army. "Don't start your Army career off by giving the First Sergeant a problem." Just because I have trouble spelling, doesn't mean I am stupid. I let the guys know the news, and passed on the advice of the First Sergeant. We took it to heart, and we all made E5 before we got out. When they got to Germany, they were split up, too; so much for the buddy system.

The USS Mitchell

January 6, 1965

PFC Knocker reports to the transport officer on board the USS Mitchell. There were two PFCs on the ship. The rest were 5000 PVT E2s enroot to Vietnam, Korea, Japan, and points west. I think there may have been a couple Sergeants up on the cabin deck, but we never saw them. We were ordered to watch over this hoard, and let the crew know if we had any problems.

By the end of the second day, there were no problems. Everyone was in their rack sick. He and I spent most of our time on the deck hatch reading Catch 22 and thinking Joseph Heller had it about right. On day 6 we arrived at Pearl Harbor. My mother's Uncle Walter, a ship's captain, lived on the Island. Mom told me to look him up when I got there.

I walked up to his house from the base. The housekeeper answered. I introduced myself and asked for Uncle Walt. In her best broken English she says, "He gone, bye now." So much for living it up in Hawaii. Next stop Guam, Wake Island, and Japan. I liked Japan. I intended to spend some R&R there, but that never happened.

One day out of Yokohama, crossing the Yellow Sea, I was hit in the face with an awful stench. I asked a sailor on the deck what that smell was. He said, "Brother that is Korea." It was 20 degrees and snowing at Inchon when we arrived.

Chapter 5

Korea

Korea: what is there to say about that war-torn country? The land was awful; devastated by the war that had ended 12 years earlier. My Uncle had fought there, and had been wounded. The stories he told, when you could get him to speak about it, were troubling. He had lain behind a 6 foot stone wall for 2 days while an ammunition dump was blown up in front of them. The wall was 2 feet high when it all stopped. He didn't get a scratch. Then he was side swiped by a diamond T dump truck and his leg was split from the crotch to the knee.

In the hospital he was in a ward with guys with broken bones. The cast would make them itch. The guys would use a coat hanger to run down inside the cast to scratch the itch. Uncle Jim said it nearly drove him crazy, because he couldn't scratch due to his leg being split open. He always said he hated dump trucks because of that incident.

We arrived at Inchon about the 28th of January, 1965. They said it was 20 degrees. All I knew was it was damn cold. All I had on was a field jacket and fatigues. We went ashore in the same barges that the troops did in the Inchon landings. They took us to a warming tent, took our orders, and began in-processing. Nobody tells you anything in the Army. They look at orders and point you in a direction, and say, "Go over there." You grab your duffel bag and go. I was being sent to the

38ᵗʰ Brigade Unit at Camp Page. They put us in a truck and we were transported to the Seoul train station. I was given the orders packet and instructions for the train to Camp Page.

Seoul was devastated by the war. It had been rebuilt on what was left of the bombed-out foundations of buildings. Every building had a line of old and new construction, running two to four feet high, jaggedly along the sides.

Koreans are industrious people, very polite and grateful for our being there, for the most part. Just don't piss them off. They are like Americans in that sense. On arrival at the Seoul train station, I took the group of guys going to Page, and went in. The first thing I saw were two Marine gunnies standing in the lobby in their dress blues. I have always had the greatest respect for the Marines. The family had lost my uncle on Okinawa in WWII. I was the first born after that, and got his name. I think they sense these things, or maybe the respect just shows. They came to my rescue, and got me and the troops on the right train.

The Kimchi trains, as they were called, were civilian passenger narrow gage commuter trains with open sides. They looked like they were constructed from 55 gallon mow-gas drums, as did all the civilian vehicles. There was very little wasted by the Koreans; they reused everything. This particular train was the local. That meant that it stopped at every village along the way. At every stop someone and his or her goat, duck, or chicken, got on or off. They all smiled and bowed, and giggled, as though they knew something I didn't. The trains were heated with small coal heaters, several to a car. It was good, I guess, that the sides were open. It was still a very cold trip. When we got to un chon ie, the city next to Camp Page, there was no one there to meet us. I asked A Korean police officer for directions to Camp Page. He pointed down the hill. I could make out the lights of the main gate through the fog.

HQ Battery CAMP PAGE KOREA

"Sir PFC Knocker reporting with three replacements from Inchon." "Well done, Private". "First Sergeant, take charge of these men and see to their billeting."

With that started my tenure with HQ Battalion, 38th Brigade, Camp Page, Korea. Our unit patch was a fist holding lightning bolts on a red back ground. It was affectionately known as "the fist of shit."

After being settled, in we reported to the First Sergeant for orientation. The first thing out of his mouth was, "You men are restricted to the post for 21 days. Any questions?" "No." I said having received this heads-up from the Marines back in Seoul. The question came from the E2 to my left. "Why, First Sergeant?" "Well, private, we are going to make sure that you don't bring anything into our village that might cause anyone else a problem. You will be medically cleared before we let you lose in the village. Is that plain enough Private?" "I'm not sick, Sergeant," came the complaint. "What does your serial number start with, Private?" "U.S., Sergeant." "That figures. PFC Knocker, what does your serial number start with?" "R.A., Sergeant." "Why do we restrict incoming replacements to base for 3 weeks, PFC Knocker?" "To combat the spread of V.D. First Sergeant." "Now do you get it, Private?." "YES, First Sergeant!" "PFC Knocker you are assigned to Battalion Motor Pool. Report to the Chief Warrant Officer, ASAP. By the way, we are undergoing a Command Maintenance Management Inspection." "OUCH!" was my reply. "Yeah, get going."

The Chief Warrant Officer, a large man, easy-going except he demanded excellence and valued initiative in solving problems. He was tall, in his late 40s I guessed. Heavy set, he reminded me of my great grandfather in his demeanor and wit.

My great grandfather was a Methodist pastor with a dislike of cats. When we were boys, on Saturdays, my uncle, cousin and I would walk the 2 miles to his home, and work for him and great Grandma Nellie. We stacked wood and tended the yard. Our reward for this was to get to sit on his lap and tell him how life was going. He would open his roll-top desk, take quarters from the drawer, and place one in each of our hands, while making some joke that Nellie would invariably say, "Now Charles, don't tease the boys!" After that, we all sat down to the best dinner anyone ever ate. It was all cooked on a chrome-plated wood stove. Everyone should experience food cooked on one of those old stoves.

Two of my friends at Camp Page were Bert and Ernie. They were two draftees out of Texas. You never saw one without the other, and never spoke of them to others without using both names. They were battalion welders; great guys. We were together at HQ for about three months, and then I was sent to Alpha Battery to fix their motor pool. It was like watching Laurel and Hardy with Ernie being the Hardy of the bunch. Once after a rowdy night in town, they spotted a Korean farmer with an ox. Ernie slipped the farmer a couple of hundred won, and then rode the ox to the front gate of Camp Page with the Korean farmer running after him. The MPs at the gate were laughing so hard that they just waved him through. We all thought we would be standing tall in front of the Colonel after that one, but nothing ever came of it.

Chapter 6

Army Script vs. Greenbacks

The United States Army is a . . . how do I say this without sounding disloyal? No! I won't say it. I'll just tell you the scam and you can decide what the adjectives are that best describe the monetary policy practiced by the U.S. Government.

We were paid in military script, funny money; this stuff was about the size of Monopoly money. It was half the size of the U.S. dollar. The exchange rate for a greenback on the Korean black market was about 1,300 won to the dollar. The exchange rate for military script was 270 won to the dollar. OB Beer in the village of Inchon-ni was fifty won, or 5.4 beers to the dollar of script. If you had a greenback the exchange rate in the village was 1300 won to the dollar, or 26 beers to the dollar. The military was ripping us off! It was a violation of the UCMJ to have greenbacks in Korea. They used the excuse that the commies could get our money and counterfeit it. Yeah, right! It sounded stupid then, too.

To be fair, instead of $200 a month, I should have been paid $962 a month in military script. Good luck with that!

The C. M. M. I.

Battery A had flunked their Command Maintenance Management (C.M.M.I.) inspection. The battery commander and motor sergeant at Battery A were relieved. I was sent to fix the problem in the motor pool as best I could, and wait on the new motor sergeant. I had been promoted to SPC. E4. My orders from the chief warrant officer were to deadline every vehicle in the battery motor pool if I had to, and to take no crap from anyone. He was still my boss 'til the thing was fixed.

What I found when I got there was a 5-ton wrecker driver with short-timer syndrome. There were two privates who knew nothing, and one civilian local, Mr. Kim, who knew everything. I don't think the previous motor sergeant let him do anything. We had eighteen, duce and half REOs, including six new multi-fuel diesels, two three quarter ton trucks, and a couple jeeps.

There was also the reason I was sent to Korea in the first place. I was a track and wheel mechanic. Because this unit had a front loader tractor, they needed me. The thing had a bad hydraulic pump. As a critical part of the unit T. O. & E, It needed to be dealt with, to pass the C. M. M. I. inspection.

I don't know why things are this way in the Army, but they are. This vehicle was critical to their mission. Therefore, if it broke down, the parts had to be "blue streaked." That means in three days the part needs to arrive at the unit. If it does not arrive, it has to be reordered. I was at Battery A about 8 months; that part never arrived. It was reordered about one hundred times. If you take the worst case scenario, sometime after I came back to the states, one hundred hydraulic pumps arrived at I Core Ordinance, earmarked for a little unit near the D M Z, with my name on the requisitions.

It was not until I received my final discharge from the U.S. Army, that I quit worrying about that loader. Maybe that's why I never got my good conduct medal.

When they reviewed my service records for the medal the conversation probably went like this: Knocker is up for the

G.C.M. He has all those letters of commendation. There is the lady he helped save giving blood, and that excellent driving thing, from the major, that captain in Korea, what do you think? Well there are those 100 hydraulic pumps he had sent to that unit in Korea . . .}

Within the week I dead-lined every vehicle in the motor pool except eight, the six new trucks and the Jeeps. Within two weeks, we were ready for the inspection. Every vehicle in the motor pool that was not dead-lined was in tip-top shape. The current blue streak pump requisition was in the file.

They arrived around noon, on the day of the inspection. The Chief Warrant's Jeep came through the gate. I was standing in front of the motor pool office. As the Jeep came to a stop, I noticed the telltale noise of metal on metal from the right rear wheels. After greeting our visitors, I informed them that their vehicle was going to be dead-lined for faulty wheel bearings. The Chief Warrant looked at me with a big smile on his face. He took a look at the vehicle then turned and said, "Good boy." We immediately took the vehicle into the shop to replace the bearing. The inspection went off without a hitch. The motor pool had finally passed its CMMI. This is a great relief to the battery Commander Capt. Smith, who had taken over from the previous battery commander.

Captain Smith was a tall lanky hard-boiled captain who was up for major. He had a booming voice and could be heard audibly when he was speaking in a normal voice from the orderly room to the motor pool a distance of about a football field length.

On one occasion I was down in the motor pool going over some vehicles. I heard Capt. Smith say, "Specialist Knocker." I turn around to look. I could not see him anywhere. I said, "Where are you sir?" I kept looking around at the vehicles.

I could not find the Captain, and he said again, "Specialist Knocker, I'm right here." I kept looking around, bewildered. "I'm here at the orderly room," he said. I looked up and there he was standing 100 yards away, halfway out the orderly room door. "Come up here, I need you," he said. So off I went, shaking my head. It was well known that he was the only man in Korea who could make himself heard on a field phone from the DMZ to Pusan.

His only other real quirk was that he loved to come down to the motor pool, pickup anything, hold it up in your face, and say, "What is this?" You would have to tell him what it was, and why it was sitting around. Usually it was some part meant to go on a vehicle that was due for some maintenance.

When our motor Sergeant arrived (his name was also Smith), things changed. He was no relation to the Captain. Sergeant Smith cured Captain Smith, of this kind of activity. After Sergeant Smith had experienced several of Captain Smith's question-and-answer sessions, Sergeant Smith had me charge up a coaxial capacitor. This is done by taking a capacitor from the distributor of a vehicle and letting the spark plug wire charge it up. This puts about 50,000 volts into the capacitor. There is little or no amperage involved, so it can't hurt anybody. But it'll give you quite a jolt. We laid the capacitor on the windowsill in the office. Sure enough Captain Smith came down and spotted the capacitor, sitting on the windowsill. He picked it up and got the biggest shock of his life. He took one look at Sergeant Smith and left the office. We never had trouble with the Captain again.

Sergeant Smith was an old Army salt. He been up and down the ranks so many times, his field jacket look like a railroad track. At this point he was a Buck Sergeant. He had been a Master Sergeant. This was probably his last tour before retirement.

To say the man liked to drink was an understatement. One could tell how drunk he was by the angle that he was walking. The drunker he got, the more he tended to lean to the left. On Saturdays, about noon, we all pooled our beer ration. We would get a case of beer at the PX and stick it in a garbage can. Sergeant Smith showed us how to use a CO_2 fire extinguisher to cool the beer. We spent Saturday afternoons drinking beer and telling stories. Every Monday, we would recharge the fire extinguisher at the camp fire station.

The end of Fear

When I was at Battery A for several months, something happened to me that I have never forgotten. I seemed to lose all fear. Prior to that, I had a healthy sense of fear; I would say normal in all respects. If I came across a poisonous snake, I felt a rush of fear like anyone else. I avoided the situation, but I would be on guard against snakes for the rest of the day. After this incident, I would just kill the snake and move on, not giving the situation another thought. I mention this because of the events in my life that happened after that, when people asked me why I wasn't shaken by this event or that. It all goes back to that night in Korea.

I was sleeping in my bunk. I guess I was dreaming. I was in a struggle for my life; someone was holding a knife to my throat. I woke with a start when the door to the hooch slammed. One of the Koreans went out towards the shower. That's when all fear left me. I don't mean to say that I am not concerned with danger, but when confronted with a dangerous situation, I tend to react to it without hesitation. This has saved my life, and the lives of those I was with, on several occasions.

During the monsoons of July 1965, I was driving Captain Smith, our Battery Commander, to Camp Page, for a meeting with the Battalion Commander. It was raining and the dirt road along the Han River it was muddy. There were small slides everywhere. As we were driving along, Captain Smith, who was watching for slides, saw a large boulder start down the side of the mountain. He yelled at me to stop. I looked up and saw the boulder coming. I gunned the Jeep, driving over a small slide in front of us. The bolder hit behind us right where the Jeep would have been had I stopped. The Captain was screaming at me. I just turned to him and said calmly "Captain, would you rather be *dead*?" We drove on in silence to Camp Page. That night, the road back was still blocked. The Captain took a helicopter back to Battery A. I was left to drive the Jeep back when the road reopened. The next day all of HQ Battery, except for the battalion motor pool, was literally under water.

The great Camp Page flood

In Korea, during the monsoon season, it rains for weeks. The year that I was there, the monsoons were particularly bad. It was raining and helicopters were grounded. Captain Smith needed to get to Camp Page urgently and ordered me to drive him. By the time we got to Camp Page, we were cut off from returning due to the flooding of the Han River. The flooding got so bad that Camp Page eventually began to flood. Water was rising so fast that we were all ordered, to the high ground, of the motor pool. All the Quonset huts were flooded along with the supply room, and orderly room. We had been ordered out so quickly that a lot of the guys lost a great deal of their personal property. We lived up in the motor pool for about three days until floodwaters subsided.

We spent the next few days drying out, and cleaning gear. The arms room got flooded, so all the weapons had to be dismantled and soaked in solvent. We cut 55 gallon drums in half, and made stands. We took all the weapons apart and put each part in a separate drum of solvent. Each guy went down the line taking parts and reassembling a weapon. It worked well and only took about a day to get them all combat ready.

I slept on the canvas of a deuce and a half. We set up emergency mess at the motor pool. We mostly ate C rations. I didn't like the coffee in the C rations, so I saved it up, and made a deal with one of the locals through the fence to trade the coffee for some Yuk juk wine. It is a kind of rice wine, very powerful stuff. Several of us sat up on top of the deuce and a half and drank a bottle of this wine. The bottles were about 4 feet tall, and held about a gallon. I was so sick the next day I could hardly stand up. The chief warrant saw me. He looked over the top of his glasses at me. Then giving me a knowing look, told me to go to the back of the motor pool bay and light the Harmon Nelson heaters. I think he knew what this would do. The minute I turned the gas on those heaters, I started throwing up. I managed to get the heaters lit, but I was lying back behind the shop with the dry heaves when the chief warrant bent over me. He stuck his finger in my face and said, "That'll teach you." He walked away. I never forgot that and I never drank rice wine again.

We had several Korean military personnel attached to the United States Army, working in the Battalion motor pool. Two of them worked with Bert and Ernie learning to cut the tops out of 55 gallon fuel drums. The operation went like this: first drums were filled with water, and then you took a welding torch and cut around the top of the drum, then emptied the drum. Bert filled several drums with water. Bert, Ernie and the rest of us went to lunch. The Koreans stayed behind and decided that they would go ahead and cut tops out of some drums. I guess they forgot the first three drums were filled with water. Instead of filling up new drums with water, they began to cut the top out of one of the other empty drums. There was a violent explosion and both were nearly killed.

Chapter 7

Fort Polk, LA

After my tour in Korea, I was sent to Fort Polk, LA. I was assigned to CO B Special troops. I was further assigned to an M151A1 Jeep repair shop in the motor pool. Now, I am 6'5" tall with hands like frying pans, and I am a track and wheel mechanic. I am trained to work on large vehicles, so naturally the army assigns me to work on the smallest wheeled vehicle they have.

To make matters worse, the new vehicles they received from the vendor, were all missing a bolt for the master cylinder, which is located under the dash and up behind the steering column. There were 93 of these vehicles. The motor sergeant, an E7 Sergeant First Class warned me about two things. One, He did not like grease on his shop floor. Two, there was a crack in the floor next to the desk in the office. In the crack, was his pet cockroach, a black monster about 4" long. He put crumbs out for it daily. We were not to harm it in any way. I was a Sp4. There was a Private E2 in the shop, about 4' 10" with tiny hands, who could install one of those bolts in a half hour, if that. This sergeant assigned me to putting in the bolts. It took me all day to get one in.

After about two weeks of this, I requested a transfer to the base MPs. They needed a Sp4, for a Guard Commander in the post stockade. I got the job. For the next several months,

I was sitting at a desk booking and releasing prisoners. Along about the 4th month of that I landed in the hospital with mononucleosis. I was delirious for a week. When I came to, I was reassigned to light duty as a driver for GTA motor pool. All I did for the rest of my hitch in the Army was to drive VIPs for the Commanding General.

When we weren't doing that we were Honor Guard at funerals or chasing prisoners for the MP's. It was the best duty you could get. Those VIPs loved to write letters of commendation. There was lots of TDY, and rank came fast. I made SP5 two months later. There were three of us that hung around together. The sergeant, the post commander's regular driver, an Sp5, and me. I guess the best story I could tell about that was the day the Sergeant showed up with a brand new lime green GTO convertible. We were all sitting on the steps of the barracks trying to figure what we could do that day. The Sergeant pulls up and shows off the new car. We ask to go for a ride, but he says he wants to take it out alone for the first ride. He says he would be back in an hour. So we agree to wait till he got back. I think he wanted to show it off to a girl over in De Ritter. After a couple hours, we were ready to give up on the idea. He finally showed up with the front end of his brand new car crumpled. He and the car were covered in cow poop. It seemed that he was tooling down the back road to De Ritter with the top down. He came over a rise, and he hit the ass end of a cow that happened to wander into the road. He killed the cow. The famer saw the event happen and promptly presented The Sergeant with a bill for the cow.

We all thanked the sergeant for not involving us in his little mishap. One of the guys asked how he was going to explain this to his daddy. "My dad doesn't have to know," was his first response. Then came the retort, "No, we mean the Post Commander." "Crap!" comes the response. "I showed the car to him this morning, and I know that will be the first thing he says when I pick him up. How's the new car?" I'll have to say, "That crappy thing?"

Getting out

About two months before my hitch was up, I came down on orders to Vietnam. The Sergeant and I were to go with the Post Commander. He was to take over the top job in Vietnam. Up to this point, I was considering staying in the Army.

Just prior to getting the orders, I was asked by one of the generals and an aide what I thought of the war. I told them I thought it was a mess we never should have gotten involved in. I was surprised when I got picked to go along. I fully intended to go with them at the end of the month and started clearing post.

The process was; you were taken off all duty, and every day there was a list of appointments such as medical shots, personal, Post Exchange, laundry, all to make sure that you were ready for deployment. There were about 30 stations and 20 days to complete the process. My plan was to go to Vietnam and spend a month, and if I did not like it, I would not reenlist. I got all the way to the last day. I gave the First Sergeant my clearance papers. He looked at me and the papers and said, "Knocker, you are a short timer in the Army. You will need to go to the reenlistment officer before you deploy. Ask them for E6. We will recommend it for you." Now, I'm not stupid. I was 6 month in grade and barely eligible for E6 and the Army had promised me Germany. I was a heavy equipment mechanic. It was my MOS, and I could be assigned next to that MOS. I would be at least an E5 or E6 and have never worked one day in my MOS. My next commander might not like that. I figured that I would do 13 months of a 6 year hitch in Vietnam. Then I would be sent to Germany, or a tank unit in Fort Bliss, and get busted for not knowing much about my MOS. The memory of the Korea C.M.M.I. came back. Maybe that's what happened to that Motor Sergeant? I went to the reenlistment interview, and they offered the E6 alright, but no MOS change and no Germany. That's when I decided to get out and think about it. I told the First Sergeant and he said I would have to clear post all over again.

That's the army. It makes no sense.

Part Two:

River City

Chapter 8

The Love of My life

One month after I got out of the military, I was sitting in a booth at the Frost Top in White Center with a couple of acquaintances from high school. I was discussing with them my intention to reenlist in the Army if nothing turned up to keep me at home. I was sitting in a booth at the back of the Frost Top when this pretty young thing pulled into the lot.

She had her young brother in the car with her. I was never one to talk to girls much, but something hit me when I saw this girl. I stopped talking and was transfixed by this young beauty. One of the guys said, what's up with you?" I just said, "Guys, I think I'm going to marry that girl." I went out and introduced myself to her, and the next thing I knew, I was at her mother's house banging my head on the chandelier in her rec room. By November 17th we were married.

The Police reserve

I thought that being a Police Officer was one of the highest callings of man. The pay at that time wasn't much. The profession at that time was riddled with corruption. Prior to coming to the River City Police, I was a reserve officer in my home town. I saw firsthand the awful corruption that was being dealt with through a Federal corruption probe in the 1960s.

I was advised at the time by one of the older officers to go to another department. Heads were about to roll. I took his advice and went to River City. I later found out that the situation in River City was not much better. However, the chief at that time was a good man and he was dealing with the problem. I only wish that I had trusted him more; I could have helped clean things up quicker than we did.

The first six months

In June 1969, I was hired as a rookie police officer. My training officer was piece of work.

He was a good and conscientious training officer, but he was also as political as I was idealistic. His flat spot was that he was a stickler for the law when it benefited him, yet political if that benefited him. Whatever the politicians wanted, he did. It worked well for him. He eventually became an Assistant Chief. I recognized what he was early on, and tried to align myself with a less political group. This hurt my career but I have no regrets.

To tell the truth when he was being his normal self, he was a fun guy to work with. He had the nuts and bolts of policing down pat. He was one of the best teachers of patrol tactics I have ever seen. I learned a lot in our time together. My worst problem in the job was report writing, and in particular *spelling*. If I was under pressure, I couldn't spell my own name. I was bad and everyone knew it. It made the probation hell for me. It was the excuse they used to fire me 6 days before my probation was up in December 1969.

The real reason was that I had trusted my training officer. We were patrolling the south district. We were headed to the station at the end of 10 days on swing shift. As we approached a local tavern, we saw a uniformed police officer fall out of the door of the tavern. He stumbled into the street. We stopped and picked him up. It was the Detective Captain for the department. His uniform was soiled and looked like it had never been cleaned. He was so drunk he was unable to stand. He had been working in uniform off duty at the tavern. We took him home and dropped him off. On the way back, I told my training officer, "That was one of the most disgusting things I had ever witnessed." We were off for the next 5 days. When we returned to work another rookie and I were fired. I later learned it was because he told the captain about my reaction to the tavern incident. He used my spelling as the excuse to get rid of me. If you can't spell, people think you are stupid, at least back then they did, but I'm getting ahead of the story here.

Throwing Rocks

One of the first police all-out responses I was involved in was kids throwing rocks at cars from a large hill overlooking the roadway at a sand and gravel business on the Valley Highway. They had been doing this on and off for weeks.

One evening in the summer of 1969, we got a call and responded with several units. We raced in, jumped out of the cars, and tore up the hill. I was one of the first up the hill, and caught one of the suspects. I was leading him down the hill in hand cuffs. I came to a place where the trail ended with about a 6 foot drop. My prisoner was hand cuffed, so I held him there until two other officers arrived.

These two officers were a couple of no-nonsense guys. I was a new rookie so when they said, "We will hold him here, and you go down, then we will lower him down," I took their instructions to heart. I went to a place where I could jump to a concrete wall and walk off, on to the parking area below where they were holding my prisoner. As soon as I jumped down, I heard a thud followed by, "Whoops!" There was my guy, face down in the gravel. They said the bank gave way, but I was never sure about that. Junior went to jail for disorderly conduct and there were no more rocks at the sand and gravel business after that.

The next day at briefing I asked them what had happened. I got a question for an answer. "Did you ever fly on a "B-1-R-D?" (A reference to his days in the air force. If you asked him about the air force he would tell you he was a gunner on a B-1-R-D) The inference was that the kid took a ride on a passing bird.

"No," I said. "He did," was the answer. Hard asses you got to love them.

Now you the reader might think this was harsh and the police were just being brutal. It is time to consider the consequences of the actions of this group. Several people had been injured in previous rock throwing incidents. There was a lot of property damage. The attitude of the children was that they were just out having some fun. Now I understood this type of fun, as a kid back in the neighborhood, I had been involved in an incident of throwing rocks at passing cars. One of the kids in the group of us that was playing on a bank overlooking the street saw a car speeding up the road and decided to take the law into his own hands. He picked up a fist sized rock and pitched it at the car. The impact knocked the car off the road. Someone could have been killed. We all scattered no one was caught but it made an impression on all of us.

In the weeks prior to the time when I caught the kid, as I said before there were several other incidents with injuries and property damage. The kids had made a game out of throwing rocks and getting chased by the police. After the kid took his ride on the B-!-R-D the incidents stopped. The message was sent that the River City Police would through you off a cliff if they caught you throwing rocks at cars. It may have been illegal unprofessional and unconstitutional, but it was effective and may have saved a life.

Moral dilemmas are a bitch.

"Oh my God, is she dead, is she dead?"

In 1969, the Dodge Super Bee had just come on the scene. I was a rookie in River City. The Valley Highway had been widened. It became a place for the adventurous to test the power of their toys.

Just why we in America love cars with engines that can send us down the road at 140 mph, I don't know. We get all shook up over guns, yet ignore the machines of death that we create and allow on the roads. The effective speed limits in most states are between 60 and 70 mph. These machines kill and maim thousands every year. Even with Chicago's so called gun-free zones, in which hundreds are killed every year, the automobile kills thousands more. We want to limit the size of gun magazines, but don't even talk about the size of automobile engines.

One day, my training officer and I were sent to an injury accident on the Valley Highway. When we arrived, there was a VW pushed up against the guard rail in the southbound lanes of this four lane road. A new Dodge Super Bee was sitting about 10 feet south of the VW. The VW had two people in the front. The driver was pinned with his feet crushed on the floor. The passenger, his fiancée, had hit the windshield. Glass from the wind shield, sparkling in the lights, covered her face.

On the hood of the Super Bee was a young man in his 20s saying "Is she dead, is she dead? Oh my God is she dead?" I rushed to the passenger side of the VW. I was able to get the door open just enough to hold her. She died there with her head on my shoulder, her eyes fixed and dilated. She never spoke. It was my first negligent homicide investigation.

The driver was alive but in so much pain that seven weeks later he still did not remember the accident.

The investigation revealed that the Super Bee was northbound on the Valley Highway. The driver saw the road open in front of him. He decided to open it up, and see what this machine could do. He raced northbound on the Highway. As he came into the curves, he crossed the center line and struck the southbound VW head on. They never saw him coming. She was starting her life a budding young school teacher; they were soon to be married. It all ended in a heartbeat. **OH My God Is she dead is she dead?**

A Scream in the night, Dec 15, 1969

I was on swing shift on a cool but rainy night. I was on south 3rd street. I heard a blood curdling scream. It sounded like it came from the downtown area. I reported this to Control and started checking alleys. We had several killings in and around River City, and we believed that a serial killer was at work. Not finding anything, I ended my shift at 11 pm.

The next day, I learned that a young woman had been found by the river, several blocks north of where I had heard the scream. Shortly after this incident I was fired by the department for the reasons mentioned above.

Three days after being fired From River City I sat down with the Chief.

The Chief was a good and fair man, but not a strong Chief. Most of the time, the assistant chief and his brother ran the department. At times he could be very assertive, but this was not often.

He had agreed with the technical reason for my dismissal. He was aware of the real reason, and wanted to encourage me to fix my spelling problem. He asked me if I had heard of a program at the community college. There was a program that could help me. The Chief assured me that if I could complete the program and pass his spelling test that he would bring me back. I was his diamond in the rough, as he called me. I determined not to let him or myself down. I started community college and enrolled in the Spelling Lab. After a year of classes, and working on my spelling, I returned to the city and retook the entrance exam. I took a spelling exam given me by The Chief, and was reinstated as a police officer for the city on February 15, 1971.

I continued my education, graduating from Community College with a two-year degree in Police Science. I entered the university, where I received my Bachelor's Degree. I continued a year into the Master's program, trying to get a Master's in public service. After the first year, I was unable to get by the statistics part of the program and dropped out.

The Detective Captain tried a couple of times to get me to do things that would've gotten me fired again, but I had the protection of the Chief and it didn't amount to anything. On one occasion he had a lieutenant and a sergeant, come to me and tell me to go to the liquor store and pick up a package for them. It was rumored that this group was getting free booze from the manager of the liquor store. The liquor store manager would write it off as breakage. I told him to go do their own dirty work, and went out on patrol. I had heard from several officers that he was out to get me. I wasn't about to let him. They were scared to death of me because of my stance on this sort of thing.

Part Three:

The come back

Chapter 9

The Return

April 20, 1971, I was back on the River City Police force when the two boys mentioned in the previous chapter went missing south of River City. They were found on April 22 murdered.

The detectives were already investigating a serial killer operating in the South County area. We had several killings in River City. One of these investigations turned up a knife with initials on it. This would later figure in the arrest of a serial killer, and the end of the career of the Detective Captain

During the interrogation of the boys' killer, the Detective Captain slipped a bug into a desk drawer in the interrogation room. Fortunately, this was spotted by two of our detectives working the case. They immediately informed the defense attorney of the device. The defense attorney went to the prosecutor. It culminated with the resignation of The Detective Captain.

There were a lot of high fives and back slapping oh goodies, when he resigned. He had been using the bug to listen in on locker room conversations and punish those that expressed decent.

Several years went past. I was working the central district when I got a call to an accident in the southwest district. When I got there, I found two cars. One had run into the back end of the other. Driving the vehicle that was at fault was The Ex-Detective Captain.

He was drunk, and sitting behind the wheel of his vehicle. I called my immediate supervisor, and asked him to come to the scene. I instructed the Captain to stay in his vehicle, while I talked to the other driver. I was off getting the subject's information when my sergeant arrived.

About a minute after my sergeant arrived, the Ex-Detective Captain got out of his vehicle. He stumbled towards me and the sergeant. The victim looked at the Ex-Captain, and said "That man is drunk!" My sergeant said, "Yes he is," and instructed me to arrest the Ex-Detective Captain.

All the way to the station, the Ex-Captain was looking at me. He wanted to say something, but knowing I was the last guy in the world likely to give him a break, we never spoke. At the station, I turned the booking and Breathalyzer over to my lieutenant. The news of this arrest had spread around the station. There were a number of the Ex-Captain's former victims anxious to see what payback would be like. So much so that Lieutenant covered the cameras and jail windows, So that the other officers could not watch on the monitors No one ever said anything about the arrest, but for about a week the guys would stop and just look at me and smile knowing that I would never discuss the matter. My sergeant took care of the explanations. My report was detailed and clear; the Ex-Captain had done this thing to himself.

I can't tell you how many times in my life when someone who had set out to hurt me had their life impacted in a very negative way. I never had to do a thing. I have always thought that God has been watching over me.

It's uncanny the way this has worked in my life. When I was about 14, I was at my cousin's house attending a party for my cousin. I was standing in the middle of the living room, when one of the guests, an 18-year-old friend hers, walked up to me and punched me right in the face. He was quickly subdued and thrown out of the party. Sometime later, this same individual was killed picking a fight with another kid by the name of Knocker, of whom I am no relation. He struck this other Knocker, as he did me. This Knocker guy struck Mr. Sucker Puncher, in the side of the head with a beer bottle he happened to be holding at the time. The bottle broke, cutting Mr. Sucker Puncher's throat. That Knocker guy got 5 years for manslaughter.

On another occasion two young toughs at the junior high cornered me at the bicycle rack and tried to pick a fight. I convinced them that would not be a good idea. Two weeks later both of them were nursing broken arms, and I didn't have a thing to do with it. I can recount many other incidences that occurred like this and have concluded that I don't have to get even with anybody. God will do that for me.

I've also had several miraculous escapes from certain death. The first when I was about eight years old. I was riding a bike down a hill, when the chain slipped off the sprocket. I had no brakes. I careened down the hill at about 50 miles per hour when I came to 16th Avenue. Two milk trucks were passing each other in the intersection. I went right behind both of them. I was able to bring the bike to a stop about four blocks later. I contribute that to divine intervention.

Don't forget about my near-miss tale of the runaway boulder that nearly missed the Captain and I on Han River Road back in Korea."

The family fight and Mr. D

I was working the 2 Robert 7 district. It was in the early 70s before we changed from revolvers to the 9 mm Smith & Wesson. I was dispatched in the early afternoon on a bright warm spring day to a family disturbance. The husband was a local contractor. He and his wife had been arguing and she wanted him out of the house. I have to say that he was a reasonable man most of the time. My partner and I arrived to find him standing in the driveway outside the residence. The conversation with him was pleasant. The disagreement he was having with his wife had to do with the fact that he had been drinking the night before and come home late. It had apparently been the last straw because the wife had served him with divorce papers. From time to time we could see the wife and his son looking out the window through the curtains.

The man was adamant that he did not intend to leave voluntarily. There were two officers at the time, myself and the other district car. During the conversation the man informs me that there weren't enough officers there to arrest him. He said I should request additional backup.

I contacted my Sergeant and advised him of the situation. The Sergeant at the time was acquainted with the man. They were, in fact, personal friends. We continued our conversation, two officers and the suspect, speaking to one another as though we had just left church. When my Sergeant arrived he was greeted like an old friend. The situation was explained to the Sergeant.

The Sergeant advised the man that it would be in his best interest to leave. The conversation went back and forth with little movement in the man's position. He was not going to leave voluntarily. The three of us gathered around him. The sergeant was on his right. I was on the left. The backup officer was standing directly behind him. The sergeant reached out and took him by the right arm and said, "You're under arrest." The man grabbed the Sergeant by the arm and threw him face down on the ground. As soon as this happened the two of us grabbed the subject and wrestled him to the ground. The three of us wrestle around on the ground attempting to get handcuffs on the man. At one point the man was lying on his back with me on top of him and the other two officers holding his arms attempting to roll him over to get the cuffs on. I moved off so that they could accomplish this. I noticed a Smith & Wesson 357 Magnum lying on his stomach. I yelled to the others, He's got a gun!" and came down with my elbow in the solar plexus. This took the fight right out of him. I quickly realized that the gun was mine. It had fallen out of my holster.

The man was cuffed and standing on his feet by this time. He said, "What did you do that for"? I immediately apologized. I was then assigned to transport the individual to the booking area at the jail. All the way to the station I was chastised for elbowing him in the solar plexus. All the way to the station I was apologizing. All through the booking process he was asking why I had to go and do that. It was not until the Sergeant came down and explained to him that it was an honest mistake. He agreed that he was as much to blame for the thing as I was. His real concern was that his 15-year-old son had witnessed his father being roughed up in this manner.

Choices have consequences.

Chapter 10

Disorderly Conduct

Disorderly conduct was a legal precept that was used by the police to regulate conduct. You pretty much had to act in a civil manner toward one another while the police were around. This included things like having sex in your vehicle in the view of the public, giving the finger to police, cursing, drinking, and making noise after 10 pm. In short, anything that pissed off a citizen that the police could not get you to stop doing was disorderly conduct, and made you subject to arrest.

People were much nicer to one another when this concept meant something.

Liberals have always had a hard time with being regulated in their conduct. Over time they have successfully narrowed the conduct which can be applied to disorderly conduct to walking in the street and blocking traffic intentionally. They always cite the first amendment; freedom of speech and expression.

It is just my opinion, but I think that the first amendment protects our right to do as we ought to, rather than what we want to any damn time it pleases us. You can't have freedom without responsibility. If you chose to be uncivil (exercise civil disobedience) you must willingly accept the consequences. I believe that this is the point Henry David Thoreau was making when he said, "If the machine of government is of such a nature that it requires you to be an agent of injustice to another, then I say break the law." Be prepared to take the consequences when you do it. Changing the law to the point that it is meaningless is not the way.

When politicians stay in office too long, their kids grow up with a sense of entitlement. Some of the kids get disorderly, and then they get the police involved. The reaction of some of these parents is to use their office to change the law, so that their kids can't be "abused by police." They would rather you be abused by their kids. It is not just the elected ones that do this, but the well-connected pinheads also. There is also a group of geniuses out there usually between 13 and 25 that think all the police are harassing them all the time

I got the following take on police harassment from one of my police buddies. And I would really like to know who wrote this because it is right on the mark, and answers this age old question by all those nitwits who think all the police have to do is pick on innocent citizens.

Police Harassment,

An officer was asked why the police harass everyone.

"I would like to know how it is possible for police officers to continually harass people and get away with it?"

From the "other side" (the law enforcement side) A police Sgt. obviously a cop with a sense of humor replied:

"First of all, let me tell you this...it's not easy. In our town, we average one cop for every 600 people.

Only about 60% of those cops are on general duty (or what you might refer to as "patrol") where we do most of our harassing. The rest are in non-harassing departments that do not allow them contact with the day to day innocents.

At any given moment, only one-fifth of the 60% patrollers are on duty and available for harassing people while the rest are off duty.

So roughly, one cop is responsible for harassing about 5,000 residents.

When you toss in the commercial business, and tourist locations that attract people from other areas, sometimes you have a situation where a single cop is responsible for harassing 10,000 or more people a day.

Now, your average ten-hour shift runs 36,000 seconds long. This gives a cop one second to harass a person, and then only three-fourths of a second to eat a donut AND then find a new person to harass.

This is not an easy task. To be honest, most cops are not up to this challenge day in and day out. It is just too tiring.

What we do is utilize some tools to help us narrow down those people which we can realistically harass.

The tools available to us are as follow:

PHONE: People will call us up and point out things that cause us to focus on a person for special harassment.

"My neighbor is beating his wife" is a code phrase used often. This means we'll come out and give somebody some special harassment.

Another popular one: "There's a guy breaking into a house." The harassment team is then put into action.

CARS: We have special cops assigned to harass people who drive. They like to harass the drivers of fast cars, cars with no insurance or no driver's licenses and the like.

Its lots of fun when you pick them out of traffic for nothing more obvious than running a red light.

Sometimes you get to really heap the harassment on when you find they have drugs in the car, they are drunk, or have an outstanding warrant on file.

RUNNERS: Some people take off running just at the sight of a police officer. Nothing is quite as satisfying as running after them like a beagle on the scent of a bunny. When you catch them you can harass them for hours to determine why they didn't want to talk to us.

STATUTES: When we don't have PHONES or CARS and have nothing better to do, there are actually books that give us ideas for reasons to harass folks. They are called "Statutes"; Criminal Codes, Motor Vehicle Codes, etc...They all spell out all sorts of things for which you can really mess with people.

After you read the statute, you can just drive around for a while until you find someone violating one of these listed offenses and harass them.

Just last week I saw a guy trying to steal a car. Well, there's this book we have that says that's not allowed. That meant I got permission to harass this guy. It's a really cool system that we've set up, and it works pretty well.

We seem to have a never-ending supply of folks to harass. And we get away with it. Why? Because for the good citizens who pay the tab, we try to keep the streets safe for them, and they pay us to "harass" some people.

Next time you are in my town, give me the old "single finger wave." That's another one of those codes. It means, "You can't harass me." It's one of our favorites.

Hopefully sir, this has clarified to you a little bit better how we harass the good citizens of our town

And I'll ad this: the real citizens that you need to give the one finger wave too are the politicians you send to the state houses, who think up all this stuff for us to do, just so they can raise money for their blotted salaries. I'll bet you thought they were you friends!

Sniffing gas & garbage in the living room

I was working the 2 Robert 7 district. We'd had numerous calls to a house in the district. The family was blessed with a 15 year old son who, for recreation, sniffed gasoline.

Junior was usually gone when we arrived. Like most good parents of an out of control whelp, they always announce to the young perp, "I'm calling the cops." On this occasion, I took the time to explain, once again, to the father how we might get Junior some help. I was invited into the house. For the most part it was a tidy home. The father, a local high school teacher, was well dressed and polite. In the living room, in front of a couch, where a coffee table would normally be, there was a pile of rotting garbage. Being clever myself, I instantly knew why Junior was sniffing gas. To my knowledge, there is no law that covers this behavior." Fetishes don't harm anything "What is a little deviant sex? Well maybe nowadays endangering a child might be considered. Can we say the cause of Junior's gas sniffing was daddy's pile of garbage, or a misguided desire to get that stench out of his nose? I can, but liberal judges maybe not so much. I made my report and sent it off to DSHS. No doubt, some liberal social worker took a look at it and said "*Why* do I get this stuff?" The final result of this behavior was that the child died from the gas sniffing and I think I was the only one that gave a dam.

Disorderly conduct, Muff Diving at the liquor store, what the kid saw

I was on patrol 2 Robert 9. It was close to the dinner hour. I was thinking about grabbing a bite to eat. I was passing in front of the liquor store, when I was flagged down, by a handsome young lad about age twelve. The kid was well dressed and very polite, the sort of young man you would associate with *Leave it to Beaver*. Not the Eddie Haskell type at all. The type of kid you would associate with the Beaver himself.

"What's the trouble?" I said in my most Community Policing manner, flashing the boy a big Knocker smile. Pointing and stammering, the young man tried to get the words out. He was pointing to a yellowish 1979 Cadillac parked just to the north and to the rear of the liquor store. This was ominous to say the least.

2 Robert 9 control I have a suspicious vehicle at the liquor store, request backup. Call the liquor store; see if everything is ok in side.

The kid manages to say that there is a lady in the car being attacked by a man.

2 Robert 9, control. We may have a rape in progress, vehicle license XXX XXX. I will be approaching the vehicle.

Seeing movement from the vehicle, but not seeing anyone in the car, I moved with my weapon at the ready. I approached the car. I advanced to where I could see in the vehicle.

As soon as I saw what the fuss was about, I holstered my weapon, and advised control to slow everyone down. I thanked the young man for his concern, and told him to run along home. We would handle it from here. He had been traumatized enough, by my calculation. By the time the other units arrived, and a few citizens started to gather, the boy was safely out of the area.

I contacted the miscreants. There were four patrol cars and an unknown number of on-lookers surrounding the car. I knocked on the window and got no response. I then opened the passenger side door. The light went on in the vehicle, illuminating the scene. The perpetrators were a 50 year old woman, on the driver side with her legs spread, and panties on the floor. A 60 year old, nearly bald, little Italian man was engaged in a sex act. Well, unless you're President Clinton, it might have been something else.

We hauled them out of the car, and after chastising them for their choice of location for the antics they had perpetrated on the public, and a twelve year old boy, I wrote them each a citation for Disorderly Conduct. I wrote "muff diving" on the offense description portion of the citation.

This case came to court some weeks later. The lady declined to appear, however the gentleman did appear, much to the amusement of the Judge. The judge was looking at me over his glasses, and choking back a smile, as he called me to the stand. I testified as to the circumstances. The judge said that the offense of Disorderly Conduct had been clearly shown, by my testimony. He then asked me to read, the (muff diving) language, and asked why I had chosen these particular words, adding he had never seen this in the legal cannon before. I replied "It most particularly described the actions that led to the arrest, using the space available." *Guilty. $500.00 fine*

Chapter 11

They are All Crazy

I was working 2 Robert 9 district. I had made several passes through the shopping center. I noticed a vehicle parked under the shopping center sign on the east side of the boulevard. When I would go by the lone occupant of the vehicle he would slump in the seat. I got curious and ran the plate. It came back as an "attempt to locate." The vehicle was missing from a rental agency. It had been rented and not returned several weeks earlier.

I contacted the driver; he identified himself as a member of the CIA, and said he was active duty military. He then told me to tell the rental agency to bill the CIA for the car, as he was on orders and had diplomatic immunity. At this, I began to think I was dealing with a whack job.

About this time, he produced a set of military orders. Having served in the military, I was familiar with the look of orders. They had the appearance of being genuine, but there was something about the whole thing. I was not buying it. He had an answer for everything I said.

Being a bit of a huckster myself, I hit him with, "What does the **G B M F I C C** say about your orders?" At this he launched into a fast-talking bunch of gibberish, and I knew, I had a nut on my hands.

The G B M F I CC was a code an old Army buddy of mine from Fort Polk, LA, had made up to mock the use of Army acronyms. If one of us said that, it meant, "Let's go get a Great Big M F Ice Cream Cone," or let's get out of here. After calling for backup, I got the CIA guy out of the car. We identified him as a walk away from the State Mental Hospital. He had a sister living in the north district. We returned the car to the rental agency, and turned the CIA guy over to his sister. The State hospital was not that anxious to take him back. We dealt with him over the next year several times.

A year later, I was working 2 Robert 9. My partner was in 2 Robert 7. My partner got a call to the sister's house on a domestic. While we were talking to the sister, the CIA guy came out of the wood work. He was wearing two large knives, one on each hip like bandoliers. My partner was on his right when he pulled a knife and brought it up above his head. My partner grabbed his arm and yelled, "Knife! Knife!" At this point, CIA guy goes for the other knife. He pulled it up to stab my partner. I caught his arm and I yell, "Knife! Knife!" My partner says, "Yeah, I know, I got it." Then I said, "No! A second knife! My partner took a look. We face planted him and cuffed him up.

The state hospital wanted him after that. My partner was kind of shook up over the incident. He accused me of saving his life several times after that. "Yeah," I would say, "you are one of the guys worth saving."

There were a number of individuals living in and around the city that were referred to as 220s. A 220 Is an individual who, through no fault of his own, has some type of mental issue. These people were called 220s because in the early part of the 20th century, police officers would get a $2.20 bounty for every nut they arrested and committed to the state hospital.

These bounties are no longer in existence. However, the name associated with the mentally disabled is used as a code to let other officers know that they may be dealing with someone who does not reason in a manner that could be described as normal. The CIA guy would fit into that category. On occasion, individuals like this wandered into the lobby of the police department complaining that the government was bombarding them with radio waves, secretly listening to their conversations, etc.

Rather than calling the proverbial men in the little white coats, we generally dealt with them by listening to their complaint. We would attempt to mediate the situation in some clever way. If you could get them to believe your blarney, you could sometimes settle them down, and get them to return to some type of normalcy.

When one individual come in complaining of government radio waves penetrating his head, I listened intently, nodding in agreement. After talking to him in the lobby for several minutes, I suggested that we line his hat with tinfoil to jam these government intrusions into his head. It seemed to him like the idea had merit. He asked me for some tinfoil. The only tinfoil we had was from discarded jail meals from serving a nice lunch to the inmates. I went back to the jail and found one of these aluminum trays. I wash it off and formed it into a hat. I returned to the lobby. We fitted it inside his stocking cap. He immediately began to praise me for eliminating the radio waves. After exchanging some pleasantries, he left the area.

Another individual in the city was hearing voices coming from under his house. He decided to hook up the hose. He put the hose under his house, and started running water. He continued this practice up until the water started running over, into the neighbors' yards and the street. This became a problem. He was eventually hospitalized, but the doctors felt he was no threat to anyone or himself. He was eventually returned to his home and was given medication to control the episodes. The medication many times leads to paranoia, and patients stop taking the medication. In this case, it eventually ended badly.

I'm neither a psychiatrist nor a medical practitioner. I have no training beyond combat medic, but having experienced a good many of these individuals, some suicidal, some confused, some just plain crazy, maybe not dangerous, but crazy nonetheless, I come to the conclusion that the psychiatric community either doesn't care or doesn't have an answer for these tortured individuals.

You see them everywhere, talking to themselves on street corners, arguing with some phantom living in the woods, unable to care for themselves, and generally in need of some sort of state assistance. The state seems to be of the opinion that these individuals are better off outside of an institution. For many people, that might be true. However, many that I have dealt with, I believe, should be institutionalized. I believe that these people want to be institutionalized. In many cases they do things to bring that about. Assault, robbery, murder, you know, small stuff like that.

The psychiatric professionals and judges lean towards keeping as many of these folks out of institutions as they can. The public at large and police officers tend to want these people locked up and treated in some way.

It is an issue of raising taxes. Politicians want to; "make a difference" so that they can point to something the voters can give them an "Atta boy" about. It gets them reelected. The general fund that *should* be used to pay for necessary things instead gets spent on their pet projects. The voters do not like to vote in taxes for things that should have been handled, by the general fund. The politicians balance expenditures by letting inmates and crazies out on the streets.

This is a way of levying a tax on the victims of the criminals, and crazies they let out. They raise taxes without the general public realizing what they have done. I call it a tax because the victim is made to pay for the actions of the state. Generally if these crazies are locked up, they don't harm the general public.

I say tax us all, and stop making victims pay the price of a politician's need for an "Atta boy." Mr. Politician, We will kick you out of office when the price gets too high. The whole trouble is that we don't stand up for victims. We let politicians have their social spending without protest. What we get is the victim lottery, or the back-handed tax on victims.

I believe there needs to be some mechanism by which the true representatives of the people's will, i.e. police officers, have just a little more authority to order individuals into treatment. This authority could rest in the hands of the chief of police or the County Sheriff.

There have been too many instances where the people, affected by these individuals, are hurt. The police are called in to deal with it. They see the potential for harm. The courts and psychiatrists disagree; release them back into the population, and tragedy results. I'll give you an example:

On one occasion I found a man in his vehicle in the industrial area of the city. He had a tire iron wedged up against the back seat of his vehicle. The point of the tire iron was sticking through the back rest of the front seat of the vehicle. He had jammed the tire iron through the driver's seat into his back. He was attempting to commit suicide with this tire iron. I took him into custody. After talking the situation over with my Sergeant, he was transported to the hospital. At the hospital, I explained the situation to the doctor. I don't know whether this doctor was just a regular doctor, or a mental health expert, but he lectured me and asked, "Why are you bringing your garbage to me?"

I looked at this man dumbfounded. I said, "This man is trying to kill himself. This is the county hospital, do something!" I said it loud enough to where it got the attention of others. There was a bit of rhubarb between the health professionals. To make a long story short, the subject was admitted to the hospital, and as soon as I left, he was released on to the streets of Seattle. I don't know what the answer is to this problem, but it certainly isn't this kind of callous behavior towards the mentally ill.

How many times in the past few years has some nut shot up schools and the politicians try to divert the public's attention from their "Aw shit" to gun control.

Politicians need to learn what every police officer knows. In life, there are "Atta boys"(Your under the spout where the glory comes out); and "Aw shits (You make a mistake and you just can't correct it.)." It takes ten "Atta boys" to erase one "Aw shit." Covering up an "Aw shit" just gets you another "aw shit."

Chapter 12

Working Robberies

I was working swing shift in the 2 Robert 9 district. My partner and I were in a two-man car. During the prior month, there were a number of convenient store robberies involving two suspects. One was a white male, 30 years old, slender build. The second was a black male, also about 30, thin build. They were known as the salt-and-pepper robbery team.

Their M.O. was to come in brandishing a shotgun, commit the robbery, and leave. Their favorite targets were small convenience stores. They were robbing **convenience-stores** all over two counties. County intelligence worked out a probable time and day of the week the individuals were most likely to hit next. This information was passed on to us at the briefing.

My partner and I were northbound on the boulevard approaching Northeast 12th. We stopped for the light at the intersection. A vehicle turned left in front of us with a white male driver and a black male passenger. The vehicle matched the suspect vehicle description we had received at the briefing. They turned into the convenient store lot at Northeast 12th. We pulled in behind them, turned on the lights, and stopped the vehicle. I got out of the patrol unit as the driver came back, and contacted my partner. While my partner and the driver were engaged, I walked up to the vehicle and contacted the black male passenger. He was still seated in the vehicle looking straight ahead. As I walked up to his vehicle, the passenger window was down. I looked down into the vehicle and could see a sawed-off shotgun sitting between the passenger and the door.

I immediately drew my service revolver and stuck the barrel in his ear. I told him if he moved for the shotgun I would blow his brains all over the inside of his nice clean vehicle. Very quietly, I told him to exit the vehicle. Taking the shotgun with one hand, I took the suspect out of the vehicle and made him lean over the trunk. My partner had the driver talking to him toward the front of the patrol car with the drivers back to me. My partner did not see what I was doing at first.

Having leaned the suspect over the trunk of his car I pointed my service revolver at the back of the first suspects head. I then said, "Oh partner." He did not respond. I said it again. At this point my partner looked up and saw what I was doing. He dropped the note book that he was holding and drew his service revolver and braced the driver. The suspects were arrested and their crime spree came to an end. They were convicted of multiple counts of armed robbery.

Choices have consequences.

The Pizza Shop robbery and the stupid judge

I was working the 2 Robert 4 district. It was late afternoon on this warm summer day. We got a call of an armed robbery at a Pizza shop. The pistol-packing bad guy was described as white male about 5' 10", short hair, baseball cap, blue jeans, and a blue and white jacket. He was driving a blue late model Chevy two-door with a sticker in the rear window.

While other units on the scene were taking the report, I started checking the area motels for the vehicle. To the east was an older motel used by grooms and horse people at the race track. As I cruised the lot, there was a vehicle matching the description of the suspect vehicle. In the room where the vehicle was parked, I could see a suspect in the window matching the description of the robber. I called for back-up. When the troops arrived, we began the investigation of this suspect. He denied involvement, of course.

We were inside the limits of the rule for a show up at the scene; less than 20 minutes had passed from the robbery. We took him and another guy we suspected as being the getaway driver back to the scene. My guy was identified as the robber. We obtained a search warrant. A search of the room turned up the money and the gun.

Case closed? Not so fast. At the trial, the judge made the following 3.5 ruling. "The prosecution has more than enough evidence to convict. This case is overwhelming against the defense. Therefore, even though the police were within the rule for a show up identification, I am going to suppress the identification of the suspect at the scene. Just to be 'fair to the defense." There is no constitutional right of fairness to the defense as it pertains to the amount of evidence that the police can bring against a defendant. That seemed to be what this judge was saying. In order to be fair she was limiting the amount of evidence we could present.

This was what the defense needed. It went from "we are going to plead the case" to "full blown trial mode." Defense attorneys are not in the business of justice, they are in the business of getting their client off the hook. Judges are supposed to be smart enough to realize this fact and be truly impartial. The suppression of legally gathered evidence is lying to the jury in my opinion. It is a disservice to the public, whom we in the judicial system are sworn to protect. The idea that jurors can't be told everything that goes on in an investigation is absurd in my opinion. If a police officer or prosecutor is found to lie or gathers evidence in a manner that is illegal, charge them.

Let another jury decide their fate. I say, if an officer of the court, including the judge, jury, Attorney general of the United States, cop, clerk, whomever, is guilty of deliberately using their office to unfairly prosecute a citizen, that person should be permanently barred from holding any office of public trust. The idea that some miscreant would go free because of an overzealous investigator is repugnant. Why do we punish the victim and the public because of a mistake by a public official?

WAKE UP AMERICIA. The ruling class is screwing with you. Choices have consequences.

This case ended with the robber getting off because the jury wanted to have a clear identification. The defense implied that the other guy, the driver, was the robber.

About 6 months later, these two went down for a robbery of a woman in a parking lot with a *shot gun,* all because the judge decided to lie about the whole thing to the jury.

Chapter 13

Playing with the Kids

From the early 70s to the mid-80s there was a group of about 300 high school age youth that seemed always to be partying together. If we responded to a loud party in the Highlands at some residence, it was inevitably found to be this group of high school age kids conducting a kager. It was always the same old story. We would arrive, half of them would run. The half that stuck around gave us as much guff as they could. We would typically arrest the ringleader and the rest would go home.

On one occasion at a party on Northeast 10th St. we arrived but had a limited number of cars available. We were just going to break the party up. I arrived and entered the residence and found all 300 of them in a small house. They weren't drunk enough yet to be belligerent. I got them all into the rec room of the small house. I asked all the girls to go to one side of the room. I then addressed myself to the girls, after having the girls raise their right hands and deputizing them. I directed my new deputies to arrest the boys in the room and take them all to the jail. When the laughter subsided they did exactly that. In an orderly fashion, the girls each went and arrested the young man of her choice. They all left in an orderly fashion. They must have all escaped because no one showed up at the jail for booking. We can't win them all.

The Bench at city hall and the Mayor

Among the transgressors mentioned above was a family in the city. The name of the tune for this subgroup was, "we can do what we want because mom will protect us." There was a mom and her sister who practiced this mantra. They were white females in their mid—to late-thirties. They each had a couple kids. The older sister was the more vocal of the two. She would not take responsibility for anything the kids did.

I was called to their neighbor's house because the neighbors were having a barbeque with about 30 friends. Her son was running a lawnmower on the other side of the fence from the neighbors gathering. He was running it back and forth right next to the fence. He was obviously harassing them. I arrived and confronted the boy. His mother was not at home. The boy admitted what he was doing was intended to disrupt the barbeque. The two families had issues for years.

About the time I was going to clear with a promise to cease and desist, the mother came home and demanded to know what was going on. I explained the matter, and mom says, "No! He did not do that, they are making it all up." I told her I witnessed the violation myself. Mom turns to the boy and asks, "You didn't do that, did you?" The boy says, "No mom, I did not."

I issued a disorderly conduct citation to the boy and told her to take it up with the juvenile court.

The mom then writes a letter to the Mayor complaining about harassment of her child by the cops. The Mayor calls a meeting of the lady, the chief, and me, to sort this thing out.

I was coming in to city hall to attend the meeting when I see the Mayor talking to the lady's son and his cousin. It seems they were picking up one end of a marble bench that sat outside city hall and were dropping the bench. The mayor told them to stop, and they told the mayor to "get F *ed." The mayor exploded at me, telling me to arrest the little punks. I said, "Mr. Mayor, let me introduce you to these young gentlemen. This is the reason for our meeting here today. The mayor looked at me and said, "Officer, after you get done booking these two and haling their asses to juvenile court, go back on patrol." The Chief and I will handle Mama!

The bench had been one of his pet projects. It was donated to the city by a club he belonged to. In court I presented over 200 contact cards listing incidents the young boys had been involved with.

The mayor had some ability to make the court understand the true nature of these "at risk youth" way beyond anything that I had hitherto been able to convince them of. Am I saying he attended and influenced the trial? Or had an impact on the outcome? I'm not saying anything. The courts made the kid disappear.

The last I heard of this young man he had moved to another state. The police there had given him an attitude adjustment. He was now the proud father of a son who may be the instrument of his final emergence into the light.

Choices have consequences.

The VW chase, and roll over

One summer evening in the late-1970s I was patrolling the 2 Robert 9 area. At the intersection of Northeast 12th and the boulevard, I drove in behind the convenience-store. There I observed an orange VW with two subjects parked in front of the store. When the driver saw me he backed up slowly and began to slowly drive away.

After a while when you are a police officer, you begin to develop what we called our "Spidey sense." That's when the hair raises on the back of your neck and you get the feeling that something just is not right.

As the VW passed the front of my patrol car, I got that feeling that something wasn't quite right.

I turned and began to follow the VW. We had gone about a block and a half when the VW began to accelerate. He accelerated to about 45 mph in a 25 mile speed zone. We were southbound. I turned on the lights and hit the siren. The VW sped up to about 50 mph and took the corner onto Northeast 10th St. eastbound, and then northbound on M Street. At this point, I informed control that I was in pursuit.

The vehicle came to Northeast 12th and turned eastbound on Northeast 12th. The pursuit went through the housing area and then back out onto NE. 12th St. westbound. As we went over the hill toward the boulevard, the vehicle speed topped out at 60 mph. The vehicle went through the intersection at Northeast 12th and the boulevard. It crossed the intersection of K Avenue. The driver then turned into a shopping center on the South side of Northeast 12th behind the post office. As he entered the parking lot, the VW driver hit the curb flipping the VW onto its top.

The vehicle slid along on its top with a shower of sparks like two rooster tails emanating from the roof of the vehicle as it slid through the parking lot. About 20 feet into the slide, the passenger door came open and a large woman fell out onto the pavement. She bounced away to my left. The vehicle continued another 30 feet. The driver magically appeared out of the vehicle. He started running westbound through the lot. I drove up alongside him. With my left front fender of the patrol vehicle I was able to knock him over.

Stopping my patrol vehicle, I was able to get out and handcuff the guy like a cowboy throwing a steer before he could recover. Throwing him into the back of my vehicle I went to check on the woman who was sitting in the parking lot 50 feet to my rear.

I asked if she was hurt she said she didn't think so. She was able to get up and walk around. I took her and put her in the backseat of my patrol vehicle. I called for backup and impound. After getting the driver's identification, I ran his name. The suspect came back clear with an expired license. I asked him why he was running from me if all he had was an expired license. At this point the driver says, "What? I should have a felony warrant for my arrest." After extensive inquiries were made through the county, it was determined that no such warrant existed.

You have to understand that the county was large with an understaffed sheriff's office at the time. Occasionally, they would make an arrest and did not get to the paperwork in time for prosecution. At such times, they would just drop the charges. Sometimes they would tell the person, and sometimes they forget to do that. I believed this was one of those times when they forgot to let the individual know that he was no longer the subject of a felony prosecution.

This young man had been under the impression that he was going to be arrested and imprisoned for two years prior to my encounter with him. When the young man learned that he was no longer the subject of this felony investigation he was much relieved and extremely happy. That is, right up until the time I told him that, although he was not the subject of the previous felony, he had just committed a *new* felony in attempting to elude a police officer. "Nobody likes criticism especially constructive criticism."

But, choices have consequences

Teach the neighbors to write reports, Surprise they can fight back

In the late 80s I was working in the detective division in property crimes. That meant I got all the burglaries, vandalism, thefts and neighborhood disputes.

At that time there was a juvenile male; he was 14 or 15—years-old. He was a particularly nasty young man who seemed to take great delight in harassing his neighbors. His main weapon of antagonism was to throw dog feces on the roofs and doorsteps of his neighbors. Occasionally he would damage cars by keying the paint or throwing dog feces on them.

The patrol officers would take reports and send them to the detective division for follow-up. On several occasions I made contact with the young man's parents in an attempt to get them to more closely supervise the young man. Since both parents worked and he was too old for day care, the parents were disinterested in my efforts to curtail their son's extracurricular activities.

Living on the same block with this young man was an insurance investigator who had become one of his regular targets. The insurance investigator had personally witnessed some of the incidents perpetrated by this protagonist. To solve this problem I enlisted the aid of this insurance investigator. I instructed him in the manner of writing statements acceptable to the courts. It wasn't long before I started receiving regular statements, signed by this insurance investigator under oath.

This gave me the weapon I needed to get the young man's attention. Every statement that I got from this investigator allowed me to issue a criminal citation for the alleged offense. I forward the same to the juvenile court for prosecution.

The juvenile court system is set up so that points are issued for each individual offense committed. Burglaries three points, malicious mischief one point, homicide 15 points; whatever they did, they received a point. It was sort of like military demerits at West Point. As points were accumulated they added up. If I were to send one citation alleging several violations such as vandalism, the citation would generate one point. If I sent multiple citations over a period of time for the same number of offenses, he would get a point for each offense.

When the insurance investigator started sending the complaint statements, I wrote a citation for each offense. I sent them in immediately. This gave him multiple offenses over several weeks. The juvenile court would process one offense, and then several weeks later they would issue a summons. The young man would have to appear in court. Because of the time between charges and the sheer number of charges, the court had to deal with each offense separately. Because each charge was dealt separately, the points added up and he started being locked up on the weekends.

Of course this generated a complaint that this young man was being picked on by me. When a complaint of this nature is generated, there is, quite naturally, a meeting set up between my superiors, myself, and those alleging the complaint. At this meeting, I explained to all those present that I did not have time to sit and babysit this young man. The neighbors on the street where they live were extremely upset with our suspect. The actions being taken were a direct result of the criminal acts of this young man.

I gave them this analogy. I was an artillery battery. He was the enemy. I had forward observers sending me his movements. I had him bracketed, and every time he made a move, I could lob an artillery shell to the juvenile courts and he would be pulled in along with his parents. The parents would have to take off work. This could get costly. When the realization trickled through their minds, the light went on.

The young man's fascination with disrupting the peace and tranquility of his neighborhood ended.

This wasn't the first time that I had to enlist a community to help in the restoration of law and order. The juvenile courts are afflicted with a malady I will term dysfunctional do-gooder syndrome, or DDS.

DDS causes those afflicted to be incapable of understanding the seriousness of a juvenile's behavior patterns. The victims of their criminal acts are treated as part of the problem. The prevailing wisdom of those affected by DDS is that they are the reason the child acts up. Hence we get programs such as victim perpetrator reconciliation. This is ridiculous.

I had a young man whose father was a minister. This young man was committing burglaries in a neighborhood adjacent to the church where the father was a pastor. The neighborhood being victimized was predominantly older retired individuals in one of our wealthier neighborhoods. I had been to numerous crime scenes in the neighborhood. I had taken fingerprints and had identified the perpetrator. I had submitted numerous cases to juvenile court.

Every time the young man appeared in court he would be released to his father. His father apparently had the courts convinced that he had the ability to straighten the young man out. He was repeatedly released and repeatedly returned to his father and he would repeatedly reoffend. There seemed no end to the cycle.

A meeting was called with the homeowners. At this meeting, I explained the situation to approximately 15 elderly women. I organized a round robin telephone complaint hotline directly to the office of the prosecuting attorney. Within three days I was called into the Chief's office and asked, "What the hell is going on? The prosecuting attorney wants every single case that this young man has been involved in. He wants every case that is likely to be filed, or can be filed in the next two weeks." After gathering all this information and submitting it to the prosecuting attorney, the young man disappeared from the face of the earth. I never heard from him again. I never knew what happened to him. He simply disappeared. Peace and tranquility returned to Mortgage Hill.

The DDS folks can't stand political heat from the old ladies. It is a good idea for all police detectives to keep this fact in mind and to recruit a hoard of pissed off old ladies when you have one of those "problems you would like to have disappeared."

Chasing the shoplifter at the Community Church

I was working the day shift in the Robert 9 District. I got a call of a shoplifter at the Safeway. The suspect was a tall, slender, light-skinned black man with a cornrow hair style. We arrived as the store security was chasing the suspect out the front door with an arm load of meat. He ran around the south side of the store and cut across a grassy field and right into the community church.

I was the last to arrive and was a witness to much of what happened next. Two officers were engaged in a foot pursuit inside the church. I took up a position on the west side of the church watching the west and south doors. Two other officers were on the east side watching the north and south doors. We could hear the pursuit inside. Thump, thump, thump, slam, thump, thump, thump, slam, thump, thump, thump, slam, thump, thump, thump, slam, thump, thump, thump, slam, thump, thump, thump, *and slam!* Round and around inside the church they went. I was just about to start to chuckle when there was dead silence in the church. Then boom, the southwest door burst open and out comes our runner, with the two officers right after him. They ran south on K toward 9th where we cut him off. He goes north on K, then up the side of a rockery and behind a house. There was one officer behind the house. I was on the outside of a 4 foot fence shadowing the suspect over the fence and into the next yard north. He ducks into a small shed.

The shed is storage for leftover wire fencing. By this time I have my weapon out and I am in alert mode. I confront the suspect with my weapon drawn. "Hold it, you!" I said. He is right in front of me on top of the loose wire. This will prove to be a mistake on his part. To escape, he has to ignore the fact that I have a 15 shot Smith & Wesson 9mm pointed right at him. There is 5 feet between us. There is no way to get by me, so I thought.

Now our runner is about 6' 5". I am 6' 5". He is a hype weighting about 125 lbs. I'm weighing in at about 250 lbs. in full gear. Advantage: me, I think. I don't see any weapons, so I'm thinking I can't shoot this guy. He doesn't look like he is going to give up. Bad deal; I have a gun in one hand and I can't get it back in the holster because it is a safety holster and takes considerable effort to holster. I'm not going to shoot him because that is just too much paper work and he is un armed, that is even more paper work. About now he tries to get by me by going under my legs. I start hollering for help and shove him back and down on the wire with my left arm.

It was like dribbling a basketball. Now the wire has several lose strands and they are razor sharp. He shows some blood. He tries again and again in rapid succession; more and more blood is shed. He gets slippery and finally succeeds in getting out through my legs. Our runner is in wide-eyed panic mode. All the cops are tired and he is off like a deer.

Now you may think the story ends here. Nope. We have divine intervention working for us.

Remember our runner has violated the sanctity of a church. God does not like his people messed with. The officers can't run anymore. We are too far from the cars. What comes down the road? Two joggers, who just happened to be returning to the Church from their jog, they see this bloody mess running from the police, and they decide to take up the chase, "because it seemed the right thing to do." They run him to ground about two blocks south on Northeast 9th. But wait, there is more. We show up and cuff the runner. We take two wallets off him; one has his own ID, the other has the ID for one of the joggers that ran him down.

Apparently while he was being chased through the church he decided to take advantage of some easy pickings. When we booked the runner he looked like he had been with Jesus on the cross. He had at least as many stripes. All of which I was obliged to explain in my report. Choices have consequences.

My partner gets stabbed

It was a fine warm spring day. My partner and I were working the day shift in the Robert 9 and 7 districts. We had stopped for coffee at one of our favorite haunts. We get a call to a shoplifter at Safeway. This kid a white male, thin, 5' 2", and 98 lbs. soaking wet. He was one of our regular customers. A rather stupid kid that was always doing something wrong and getting caught. He always got caught because he looked guilty all the time. There was just something about the kid that told anyone he was up to no good.

On this day, he had entered the Safeway and raised the suspicions of Safeway security. They called because he had eluded them before and was at the meat counter stuffing meat in his shirt. We arrived to see him running from the security. My partner and I took up the chase. We ran him into a grassy field where he went to the ground. The grass was 4 to 5 feet high. We could see the grass moving as he tried to crawl his way through the field. My Partner went around flanking him. My partner was an ex-Marine, very agile. He was very practiced at that flanking thing; Marine recon you know. I moved along with him, blocking any attempt to escape south. The suspect crawled along the base of a small hilly area where my partner was waiting in ambush. As he neared my partner, my partner leaped. He heard my partner and rolled over, holding a large bowie knife. The blade was up when the suspect rolled over. As my partner was coming down, he sees the knife and yells, "KNIFE!" Then like a cat, he handsprings over the kid. The knife punctured his Kevlar vest about a half inch. I was moving in on their position. I saw the knife as my partner rolled out. I slid in and disarmed the suspect by punching him repeatedly in the face. I secured the suspect and went to see about my partner. At the time he didn't think the knife went through, but when we got the vest off him, he had a half inch nick right in the middle of his chest. The suspect had about 8 welts all over his face.

The suspect was a little thief about 19 years old very small with a slight build after it was over we both felt sorry for the kid even though he could have killed my partner with that large hunting knife. He must have thought he was being chased by the store employees rather than the police. He had never given us any trouble in the past. It was his choice to be armed in the commission of a crime and his choice to run from the store security. At the time we did not know who we were looking for or we may have just called to him and talked him into surrendering. He was the kind of kid that would have done it if we had asked. He chose to light that candle and Choices have consequences.

My partner and the radar trap at race track

My partner and I were working graveyard shift in the 3 Robert 1 & 2 districts. It had been a long and slow Sunday night. Early Monday, we went to breakfast at our favorite restaurant on South 3rd St. My partner liked the pancakes there and had converted me to this new vice. When the restaurant opened, we were waiting. The pancakes were huge. Two was all any normal man could ingest at one sitting.

After finishing the meal and having nothing to do but our final building checks, we agreed that we would meet at the track to ambush some of the Monday morning speeders, which were complained about by local residence in the area. My partner set up with the radar working west bound traffic. I waited near the track. After a few minutes, traffic started flying by.

My partner was not calling any vehicles or making any stops on his own. After about ten minutes of this I went to check on him. I soon realized the slow night and pancakes had taken their toll on him. There in the moonlight was my partner, sitting behind the wheel of his patrol car. The radar gun was on the ground. The cord was running into the window, his arm was limp and hanging out side with the cord between his fingers. I could not resist. I got my camera out and took a picture. My intent was that the photo would later show up at the guild dinner dance as one of our "Aw Shit Awards." I went over and woke him gently and said we had better pack it in, it was quitting time.

Judges, homosexuals, and kids

Once upon a time there was an old homosexual. This homosexual liked boys ages 12 to 20. This homosexual was a judge for years, and he loved the juvenile court system. I started hearing about this judge in the 1970s, when I arrested a homosexual flower shop owner for the rape of a 15 year old boy. During a search of the suspect's apartment, we found a briefcase with hundreds of stolen credit cards and a .22 pistol that may have been used in robberies in the county. As soon as we turned up this item, the homosexual shop owner called a judge. I assume it was a judge because when the party on the other end of the line answered the homosexual shop owner called him *your honor.*

The conversation was brief and ended with "your honor guy" saying something that made the flower shop suspect turn red in the face. I suspect that your honor guy didn't like the fact that we were there when the flower shop guy called. That's just what I suspected.

In 1988, several years before I retired, a juvenile court judge committed suicide after being exposed as a pedophile. I'll leave it up to the reader to make the connection as to whether he may have been "your honor guy."

Over the years there have been several juvenile court incidents that reinforced my belief that something shady was going on at the juvenile court involving judges and court commissioners. Strange rulings; such as one involving a court commissioner, and a vicious little perpetrator, who was brought up on charges of intimidating a witness, in an assault case of a 72 year old lady. While he was sniffling in the chair, the commissioner said, "The police have proven their case, but I am looking at this young man with his blond hair and his blue eyes welling with tears and I can see he is remorseful. I'm dismissing the case." I jumped out of my chair and went for the commissioner. I was grabbed and restrained by the prosecutor. The commissioner left the court room. I demanded the prosecutor appeal, but nothing ever came of it.

The rumor was cry baby's mother was banging a judge. Now I can't prove that, I'm just reporting the rumor.

I don't know if there is racism in the courts but there is definitely preferential treatment of blond, blue-eyed crybabies.

Mom gets Jr's Ear at the station, bad night on the loop

On a typical Saturday night in downtown River City, the loop was in full bloom: 5,000 kids and 20 or so officers to keep them in line. The whole thing amounted to the world largest babysitting service.

All those parents sending there little tikes over to River City for me and the guys to watch; It's nice to know that they can trust us with their Rolexes.

While out on patrol about midnight, I came across a young man. He was tall for a two year old. . . about 6 feet 6 and about 160 lbs. It must have been his first trip to the Loop. His sense of decorum was somewhat lacking. He was half in the bag when I first came across him. He seemed to be in a mood to pick a fight with anyone and everyone in a blue uniform. It had long been my personal policy when confronted with children of this type to cancel their ticket to the dance and call in the parents for a consultation. That is what I did in this instance.

I called Mom and explained that her son was being difficult and was not playing nice with the other children. He was being downright disrespectful of the authorities and had said that we would be sued by his parents if we did not let him go.

"I can't believe that, not my son, he would not act that way", was mom's response. "We will be right down. See you in 15 minutes." "Ok ma'am, he will be in the front lobby."

Did I mention that I neglected to tell Junior that Mom was on the way? Well I guess I forgot to warn Junior of Mom's impending arrival. Junior was standing in the lobby of the police station with his back to the door. I was standing in front of him, looking over his shoulder, as mom walked in. Junior was in the mist of impugning my manhood, and giving the clerks in the area a French lesson, as Mom walked up behind him.

She was a tiny thing, not much more than about 5 feet tall. (This came from *her* I thought?) Mom spoke first, "Are you through with him?" came the authoritarian question.

The last time I had heard words spoken in that manner it came from a Sergeant Major in the Army. There was a moment of dead silence in the lobby. Everything stopped. The girls stopped typing, everyone froze, the young man gasped.

I had intended to have words with Mom, but knew instinctively it was not necessary in this case. "I believe I am, ma'am," was my reply. Now the young man was in somewhat of a spot. He had just impugned my manhood and was about to say something about how he was mistreated when Mom cut off the conversation by reaching up and grabbing Junior by the ear. She jerked him down to her size. Bent over double, she ordered him to apologize to me and the girls in the office area. He quickly made his apologies. Out the door he went with mom speaking right in his ear. Now everyone in the lobby is looking at me.

"Karma? I said you can't beat karma."

The guy at the gas station and the F Word

It was a warm summer evening. The children were partying and generally enjoying themselves. I was working the 2 Robert 9 district. I had responded to a loud party call, probably from some social outcast who hadn't been invited to the party.

I had been dispatched to the complaint in a large apartment complex around 10 p.m. everyone in the complex was partying.

Most of the sliding glass doors were open. The evening being warm, you would expect that.

The call was routine. (Hey cops out there, before you say "nothing is routine in police work," don't you think I know that? It's my story.

I contacted the complainant and the party goers and tried to come to some accommodation between the parties. That might have been the end of the fun had it not been for the 8 to 4 crew who had swung by to back me up.

The 8 to 4 crew's sole purpose was to be a floater car. They went where the action was. I cleared the noise complaint after getting the parties to respect each other's right to exist.

As I was about to exit the lot, I saw that the 8 to 4 crew had stopped a group of revelers in a car across from the apartment complex at the Gull gas station. There were two apartment buildings along NE 4th with their rear decks overlooking NE 4th.

About 20 feet to the rear and south of the unmarked patrol car, was a young man dancing around shaking his fist at the officers of the 8 to 4 crew. He was yelling at the top of his lungs the vilest obscenities imaginable. I let them know I was there and was observing the young gentleman.

I exited my patrol car and strolled across NE 4th noticing as I did, the young man had garnered the attention of most of the folks in the two buildings along NE 4th. There were several other groups of people coming out of the other buildings to see what all the commotion was about. The young man was seemingly oblivious to me or the audience he had attracted with his antics.

I walked up behind him and stood there and looked around at the crowd. I lifted my hands in a jester meaning, "can you believe this?" The young man still had not noticed that I was standing right next to him, just to his rear. He was still spewing out obscenities when I leaned forward and whispered in his ear, "F YOU."

He then jumped straight in the air and spun around. At this point he noticed that I was a 6 foot 5 inch police officer in full uniform and there was a crowd of at least 100 onlookers laughing and pointing at him. That's when he was overcome with religion and piety.

The young man started jumping around and yelling at the crowd while pointing at me repeating over and over "HE SAID THE F WORD." While doing this, he lost all his concentration on the 8 to 4 crew, who by this time had finished their warning of the driver of the car they had stopped. They had exited their unit and were now standing behind the young man. As he bounced around yelling, "he said the f word," and pointing at me, he happened to back up into the 8 to 4 crew. They snatched him up, one on each side of the young man, lifting him off the ground. At this point, this young man demanded to see the Sargent. "I am the Sargent," came the reply, "and you're under arrest for disorderly conduct." The crowd roared.

I know I should not have said the F word. Something came over me. The sight of this anarchist challenging authority over something he knew nothing about created an exigent circumstance.

At such times, the Supreme Court has ruled that police can act outside the bounds of decorum to reestablish public order. I have every expectation that the ACLU will forgive this slight peccadillo on my part. *Choices have consequences.*

You didn't SEE me do that. (Not; I didn't do that.)

At times when a police officer is engaged in that most distasteful of all activities that police do e.g. The disciplining the children of those who refused to do it themselves; you run across some mental giant who makes some statement that you can't help but remember.

One fine spring day while patrolling the River City highlands, I happened to see a young man doing some damage to one of our street signs. For some reason the children loved to jump up and bend the street signs over. I don't know why this is popular, but it is.

Some break them off and decorate their rooms with them.

Anyway, I see this going on, and I quietly roll up on this scene and get out of the patrol car, unseen by the young man. I walk up and say, "What are you doing?" The young man turns around and the first thing out of his mouth is "YOU DIDN'T SEE ME DO THAT!" "Oh yes I did," I said. "No! You didn't," says the young man.

"Well," I said, "how about we let someone else decide if I saw that or not. "Ok," the kid says, "I'll call my MOM." "No," I said, "we have a city arbitrator who handles these things." "Ok, call him," the young man says. "Well," I said, "I can't just call him, we have to put in a request for that." The young man agrees to put in the request, so I got my request form and wrote out the request.

I told him he had to sign the request form, which he did gladly. I did my investigative thing, took photos of the damage. It wasn't that much just bent the sign a little. Let's say $50.00 to have the guy from the city shops come out and straighten the sign. The kind of thing I would usually not waste too much time on, but my spidey sense said, this could be different, and fun to see play out in the COURT.

I was to be proved right. Sometime after the young man left my presence, someone at the police department got a call about the arbitration request, actually being a citation for malicious mischief. Of course the powers that be could see how that kind of misunderstanding could have occurred.

They ask if in the future, I could be a little clearer as to the real meaning of the request in question. I happily agreed.

Several weeks, later the young man, his parents, and their lawyer showed up in court. Let's add this all up: $250.00 bail for Mal/Mischief, $250.00 for the lawyer to come to court, mom and Dad and Junior take a day off work. City pays me 4 hours of overtime because this thing is on my day off.

I am called to the stand. I testify to the facts of the case and then the prosecutor, who has been eagerly awaiting this case, asked with a sight smirk on his face, "Officer Knocker did this young man make any statements to you when you approached him?" "Yes," I said. "What was the statement he made as you approached him?" **"You didn't see me do that."** A low chuckle comes from the audience in the courtroom.

The judge looks over his glasses first at the defendant and then at me. "Are there any questions from the defense?" "Yes, your honor." *(Mr. Attorney wants to justify the $250.00 fee he is going to charge.)* "Did you advise my client of his rights prior to this statement?" "No," I replied, "it was a spontaneous utterance." "No further questions." "Officer Knocker," the judge asks, "this is not the usual kind of case you bring into my court. What was the damage here?" "About $50.00, your honor." "Had he not taken the tact he did with you would you have brought this case?" "No, your honor." "What is your normal protocol in these matters?" "I would have taken his name and address and turned the matter over to the city shops to fix the sign, and bill him for the damage." "Interesting," says the judge.

"Well young man, would you be interested in paying the damages to the city, and we would dismiss this with cause as long as there are no further violations of the law for a year?" "Your honor, he didn't see me do that." **<u>Guilty! $500.00 fine!</u>** *Choices have consequences.*

There are moments in life when a liberal judge and a conservative police officer can see eye to eye. The lesson for young eager police is that you should always look for the opportunities in your job to render a public service. By presenting these issues to the court rather than taking affront at some mentally challenged youth, you can embrace the opportunity to exercise your creative side.

Beer in the trunk: a message to the parents

The River City Loop was always a fixture in the City. The local kids would parade their cars down Second Avenue, past the high school, and go south to South Third, and up through town, and back to Second and do it again and again until the cows came home. A lot of beer was consumed.

The dumb ones would park on the overlook, a spot on the power line road, above the church. I say the dumb ones because we could see them from almost anywhere. The citizens would call if we let them stay there too long. We could come from several directions and trap them. We would get five or six cars at a time. It was not hard to get probably cause to search a trunk, as they usually were drinking.

We soon tired of just writing them up for liquor violations. Some of us took a different approach. Under threat of arrest, booking, and impounding their cars, we gave them a choice. They could pick up all the beer bottles and trash, or go to jail. They always took police call rather than jail and home for the night. (For all you nonmilitary types, the term "police call" means a general cleanup of the area.)

If we found beer, we cracked all the bottles and cans and drained them upside down in the case. We had them take the stuff to a dumpster. By the time they got to the dumpster, the trunk smelled like a brewery. We hoped they would have to explain that to mommy and daddy. It was usually daddy's car.

Railroad cars of beer

The River City Loop was a cool thing to do when I was a kid growing up. Things were fairly quiet on the Loop back then. We had our own version of this in White Center, where I lived. We would head down around the point and back to White Center driving up along the coast. We called it ratting around. White Center came to be known as Rat City.

In the early 70s, the River City Loop was written up in a magazine and all hell broke loose. Kids came from as far as Los Angeles just to check out the River City Loop. Most were harmless, but a few were bent on trouble; the worst of these were the snobs that had rich parents. They thought they were entitled to drink and tear up the town.

I set my "crap barometer" at" 0 just for them.

The railroad siding where the train cars were parked, down town was a pain in the neck. Beer cars were routinely parked on the siding. The cars were painted with the various brands of beer they contained. The Loop was just a block away. Did they think the kids wouldn't take notice? If I didn't know better, I might think the railroad did it for a tax right off. They could allege truckloads of beer were taken and who would know.

Those cars were regularly broken into. We caught a few of them and generally knew who the ringleaders were. We made them pay by popping them for anything we could.

We told the city council how to stop the Loop in 1972 they finally did it in the 90s. After $5,000.00 in damage in one rowdy night, they simply passed a law making it a misdemeanor to circle the Loop twice. We set up check points and recorded license plates. Two weeks of this and it was over. It was no fun to come to River City just to go around the Loop once.

The girl in the bathroom at the high school dance

I was working at an off duty job at River City High. It was one of those typical school dances: lots of kids, and parents, and teachers volunteering as chaperones. The night was uneventful until about 9 pm. I was approached by one of the school chaperones, who stated that there was a girl lying on the floor of the girl's locker room.

She was non responsive and smelled really bad. The locker room had been cleared of students. An aid car was summoned and was on the way. I entered the room and observed a white female about 5' 4" laying on her face in a pool of vomit, and I detected the unmistakable odor of wine and poop. She was soaked in this mess from head to toe and the smell was awful. Holding my breath, I checked her vital signs. I determined that she was breathing, and had a strong pulse. The aid crew arrived shortly thereafter and verified my original assessment. The crew provided me with the necessary supply of rubber gloves. I was able to identify her from the ASB card she had in her pocket. I subsequently contacted her parents who were just returning from a night out.

I explained to Dad that the young lady was in no condition to be riding in the family car. The aid crew had declined my suggestion that they transport her to her home. I suggested that a pickup truck was the better mode of transportation for a situation such as this. Dad said he had one of those. He would be on the way down to retrieve his little darling. While I was waiting for Dad, I went and retrieved a wool blanket from my patrol car, along with my camera and film. I then proceeded to take a roll of photos for the family scrapbook.

When Mom and Dad arrived, I brought them into the locker room and reintroduced them to the sweet smelling object of all the fuss. Mom was shocked but Dad just looked and shook his head. Everyone was very polite and sympathetic with Mom and Dad. Dad even thanked me for having the foresight to suggest the pickup. "The least I could do." was my response. Dad and I both gloved up and rolled daddy's little girl up in the wool blanket.

We carried her gently out to the truck and plopped her in the back. It was raining. Mom and Dad both remarked that she needed a shower anyway. As they were leaving, I took Dad aside and presented him with the roll of film I had taken earlier. I explained to him that she may benefit from seeing the photos as a picture is worth a thousand words. He agreed and again thanked me for having the foresight to document these events for him.

"I have four sons," I said. "I would give my eye teeth for black mail photos like these." "Right on!" says Dad. I advised him that the blanket could be returned at his convenience. Off they went, one happy family reunited with their loved one.

About a week later, I was at briefing when I was paged to the front lobby of the police station. As I was walking out to the lobby, I met the police Chief as he was walking out. We entered the lobby together. There standing in the foyer was the young lady from the high school locker room incident. She was holding the blanket from my patrol car out in her arms like she was handing something of great value. The chief asked if that was one of our patrol car blankets. "Why yes," I replied. "Can you explain this, Officer Knocker?" "Why yes, Chief!" I explained, emphasizing Chief! This is the young lady from the River City High School locker room that everyone has been talking about. "Oh," says the Chief. "Thank you for cleaning my blanket." "You're welcome," was the squeaky reply. With that, the red faced young lady left our lives never to be seen by us again.

Again, choices have consequences.

A shooting in north River City,

The number of times I fired my weapon on duty in 28 years, not counting the range, you can count on one hand. Yet the most asked question of the citizenry is "how many people have you shot?" The answer is none.

The number I Shot at is two. One, if you don't count the time I made a young local burglar crap his pants. I shot into a stump next to him when he turned and fled the scene of a store burglary in north River City. He was about 15 at the time. We got a call of a burglary in progress at the north River City Market on Park Avenue North. About 5 cars arrived to find five or six of our local punks all over the roof and inside the store. We knew them all. My partner got out with the shotgun. We ordered them to halt. The bunch of them started running in every direction. I confronted one perp as he came off the roof and landed at the rear of the store. I drew my weapon and stuck it right in his face and ordered him to the ground. He stood there a few seconds staring at the gun and I said again, "Get on the ground!" "Knocker," he says, "you're not going to shoot me." At this point he turned to run. He headed toward a fence at the school and leaped it. As he went over the fence I thought to myself, what this kid needs is a brain operation.

My dad's cousin, a salty full-blooded Cherokee and veteran of Anzio, had used the phrase when he took me out to castrate steers at his ranch in Oklahoma. I asked him why he called that a brain operation and he said, "because I am changing their minds from ass to grass."

I pointed my pistol at a stump that was next to him. As he went over the fence I fired once, and I yelled "Missed!" He crapped his pants and caught a gear rarely witnessed by man. He was gone before I could get to the fence.

In hind sight I probably should not have done it. It did stop him from thinking we would not shoot him. The unintended continuance was that my partner was running around with a shotgun. When he heard the shot, this Marine veteran of Korea didn't know that I was giving a perp a brain operation. He thought the Smurfs were armed. My partner then delivers a horizontal butt stroke to the side of the Smurfs head that he was chasing. Then he turns and covers the area where the shot came from. I see what is happening and yell to my partner, "It was me!" A half hour later we find the perp in his bed at home still in his pooped pants, boots and all.

The only one in that family that wasn't crazy was the perp. He was just a straight up criminal. The others all had mental issues.

I was on South 3rd near the old theater on swing shift. I see the first perps brother, standing in the road at Logan Street yelling at a power pole. His VW was smashed into the pole. As I walked up to him, he says, "Officer Knocker, arrest that pole!" (He was always very respectful to me personally.) I asked him, "Why the pole?" "Can't you see, Officer Knocker?"

"That god damn mother f ing pole just smashed my car!" At this point, I took a good look at him and noticed his pupils were the size of dinner plates. He seemed a bit disassociated from reality. He then claimed, so that all of down town could hear, that "the mother f-ing pole" had come out in the middle of the street and grabbed his car and slammed the car into the pole.

I called for the aide unit. The aide car arrived and he began complaining that I was not arresting the pole. I was later to learn that the combination of plain crazy and PCP was the probable cause of the pole's inappropriate actions.

Burglary

The crime of burglary taught me that you never know what to expect with the guys that commit crimes. The first one I can remember was the winery caper. One of our detectives "developed" some evidence that one of our locals was burglarizing a winery. It was always being hit, but the suspect kept getting away. The suspect was a one legged local who was well known to the department.

This guy had several girlfriends scattered around north side of River City. He was a graduate of River City high. He had lost his leg in a motorcycle accident after graduation. The Detective had somehow gotten a tip from one of the girls that he was hitting the winery regularly. One night we staked the winery out. Sure enough, he shows up in the area. The Detective had put an alarm in the building and several of us were staked out watching the doors on the north side.

The winery was on the south side of the street. All the doors were on the north side. The suspect was seen walking in front of the building. He walked past the building. He went down the alley behind the winery. Just when we were beginning to think he had made us, we got an alarm from inside the building. We surrounded the building and he was caught sneaking out the back where he had loosened a metal siding panel and had been using it like a rear door. He had several cases of wine ready to go and was carrying one in the alley when he was caught.

The Big 5 store was often the subject of regular calls about rocks through the window.

In the early morning on our last night of the 10 day shift we got an alarm at the Big 5. Several units responded. There was a large hole in the window. The hole didn't seem large enough for a normal man to enter. We were there quickly, the first officer taped the glass with his night stick and the glass fell out. We all entered and fanned out, checking the building. I went south carrying my shotgun. Two others went center and north. Suddenly, I hear, "Halt! Drop the gun, asshole! Drop it or we will shoot!" I came around a counter to see a suspect, crouched, trying to load a 45 cal. auto behind the gun counter. Two officers had him covered from the front. I had him flanked from the side. He didn't have cover from me. I jacked in a round and yelled, "Put it down!" He looked in my direction and saw the barrel of the 12 gage shotgun I was holding and dropped the gun. He put his hands up and surrendered.

When we collected the gun, it had a fully loaded clip, inserted backwards in the weapon. We were that close to an all-out gun battle inside the store.

This taught me that things are never as they first appear. We were joking and talking about how some clerk having pissed off a regular, or some drunk had come by and found a door stop carelessly left outside and returned it. I never took a careless attitude again when going to a call. I had been wised up.

Defense plant guards and the fence jumper

It was the late 70s. I was working a swing shift in the Robert 9 district. I was backing the north cars on a chase. Everything converged on Park Avenue North near the defense plant gate 9.

As I came up, a suspect was running north on Park, along the fence, at the local defense plant. I had the suspect cut off from the north. He stopped and was bouncing around looking for an out. He had no place to go. The next thing I see is this guy climbing the defense plant fence. He is over the fence like a deer. As I get there, he is between two buildings, facing two defense plant guards. I yelled at him, "Stop! You're in a restricted area. Those guards will shoot you!"

The guards crouch and make a motion to go for their guns. The suspect freezes. I say, "Now listen guy, maybe we can get you out of this. Start backing up." To everyone's amazement he does just like I say. We back him up one step at a time with the guards playing along. I get him to the fence and halt him. "Now turn slowly," I tell him, "now slowly climb the fence. Over the top now, slowly, climb down now. Let go of the fence." We cuffed him and talk to the guards, thanking them for not killing the guy, and then the suspect thanks them too.

Sometimes things just work themselves out. I just know this guy is telling this story to his grandchildren, about how his life was saved by a quick thinking River City police officer.

The county boat chase and the bridge at the River

On a warm summer evening, I was patrolling in the area of the River City Airport. A call came in that the County Harbor Patrol was in pursuit of a small boat on the lake. The boat was headed for the mouth of the river. The patrol boat was going to lose them. They were requesting our assistance.

I was right there when the call came in and could see them coming across the lake. I assessed the situation and determined that I might need my shot gun loaded with slugs. I was thinking that I may want to sink a boat.

I located my patrol car on the airport access bridge which spanned the river to the airport. I loaded the shotgun and waited. As I waited, I thought if I put one through the bottom of the boat, I could expect to make a silver dollar size hole, and bounce the boat around a little. If I hit the seat first, I may get a bucket size hole. I then thought I could do both if they cooperated.

You don't get the opportunity to make ballistic comparisons in the field. This could be a great opportunity to further the science of ballistics.

Sure enough, they beat the patrol boat to the river. They were looking back at the boat laughing. I had the loud speaker turned on. I got their attention with a loud, "Halt!" I announced over the loud speaker that my shotgun was loaded with slugs and I was about to sink their boat.

"If you do not turn around and contact the patrol boat, I will sink your boat." I recognized the suspects as two of our local burglars. I called them by name having dealt with them before and they knew me. "You're not going to shoot us, Knocker," one of them said. "No," I said, "but I'm damn sure going to sink your boat, and sic the dog on you when he gets here if you don't turn around and contact that County boat."

They had two choices: one, contact the boat; two, try to get past me by going under the bridge. I could hear them discussing the matter. Then I hear from the boat over their speaker. "Well boys, will it be us, or him, then us"? That made up their minds. Better one charge than two and a sunken boat. They turned back and went to the County boat.

I met the boat later at the City Park and learned that the boys had been towing a stolen set of pontoons when the chase started.

I passed on my thinking as to our ability to further the science of slug ballistics. If only they had not said "Well boys, will it be us or him, then us?" We may have been able to do something great to further the science of ballistics. "Damn," one of the deputies said, "we just need better communications out here."

Car thieves and motorcycles

I kind of hate car thieves and motorcycle riders. Not as individuals, but as a class. Most are fine people. It is a fact that as a class they are responsible for more stupid than your average criminal type. They tend to make the average police officer hate his job because of all the paper work they create.

Let's put this in some perspective. Your average burglar breaks a door or window, then steals the dog and is off selling your stuff for a tenth of its value. Stupid? Yes, but the paperwork is simple. A short report and book the evidence into property. If you have a suspect you may have to get a search warrant. No big deal.

The car thief is a different story. They are thrill seekers. Dummy steals the car, rides around and drops the car. If we are lucky, it gets dropped in town and we recover it. Short report and impound, or the victim comes and picks it up. No big deal.

On the other hand, Dummy steals the car gets in a police chase involving multiple agencies, runs into Seattle, gets caught in, let's say, a Seattle trap near Green Lake, and is injured by being smacked in the nose by an unidentified patrol officer who didn't hang around to make a supplemental report on the injuries.

The River City Officer is left to explain the citizen's injuries by saying, "I don't know, Chief. Maybe he bumped his nose on the steering wheel when he came to that abrupt stop." If the chief buys it, great, if not, here come internal affairs.

Now, I would be willing to bet that all car thieves ride motorcycles. It is because they are thrill seekers. Not all motorcycle riders are car thieves however.

Back in the 80s I developed a plan to rid the nation of car thieves. The plan was to have the President announce to the nation during national car thief awareness week that only car thieves could ride motorcycles. The Army could be directed to run anyone over riding a motorcycle with a M1 Abrams tank. The collective IQ of the nation would benefit greatly. The President would surely be reelected.

It was shot down because the entire environmental activist movement would be pissed off because of the paper work it would create for them.

With all that oil and grease on the roads and highways causing more paper work, forests would have to be cut down to make the paper, and thus endangering the spotted owls. Go figure!

Now motorcycle riders that are not the car thief type have a tendency to be subject to bouts of incredible stupid. They forget that the laws of nature are not in the direct favor of your average biker. In the best of circumstances, these crotch rockets are unstable and subject to all the chaotic machinations that nature can throw at them. With this in mind, I relate my eye witness encounter of a biker versus a motorhome.

My family and I were coming home from a drive-in movie. I had come home from work and was still in my uniform when we left for the movie. I removed my uniform shirt, and had it in the car, so I was ready for business when all hell broke loose that night. As we headed down the freeway toward home, a biker passed us. The biker was in front of me in the left lane. A large motor home pulling a bike trailer was in the right lane, just a head of the biker and us. The biker was gaining on the motor home. What was to happen next was to make my kids say, "Daddy, did you see that man fighting with the bus?"

As the bike got alongside the bike trailer the motorhome was pulling, the left turn signal of the motorhome came on. I could see the danger of what was about to happen, and I slowed. The biker, however, did not grasp the potential hazard and sped up. The driver of the motorhome forgot he was pulling a bike trailer. The motorhome driver came over in front of me trapping the motorcycle.

The biker did not take kindly to the maneuver. The biker sped up alongside the motorhome, kicking the motorhome in the side. This got the attention of the motor home driver, causing the driver to look back at the trapped biker. When he looked back, the motorhome was pulled slightly to the left, sending the biker ass over tea kettle into the wild roses the state had planted in the median.

Wild roses are not the first choice of your average biker to land in at 55 mph. everybody stopped. I put on my shirt and went to work. A trooper was there in a minute and he says, "How did you get here so fast, and where is your patrol car?" I pointed to my car and said, "Do you want me to get the statements from the witnesses and mail them to you?" Thank God nobody was killed. But the biker looked like a porcupine got ahold of him.

Least you think this is a one off, I was on foot patrol at the Beach Park in North River City. A friend of my partner came by on his new Norton 700. He was out for his first ride. We talked for a while. He decided to take a spin out Lake Washington Blvd. He took off from the park entrance north bound. Several minutes later we got a call of an injury accident on Lake Washington Blvd. I arrived and found the biker sitting in the ditch in front of a culvert. The bike was totaled. He had hit some gravel on the side of the road and lost control. When I got up to him, I first thought that his leg was stuck inside the culvert. On closer examination, the fire department found that his leg was snapped above the knee and was bent back so that he was sitting on the leg. He didn't seem to be in any pain until they tried to move him.

In the mid-80s a local car thief was riding his chopper. This thing was decked out with high rider handlebars and decorated with two javelins pointing up between the handlebars.

Numb nut took off on North 6th and turned the corner on Defense Plant Drive. He cracked the throttle wide open to make the light at North 4th. A station wagon was westbound on North 4th and hit the intersection just as the bike was trying to beat the light. Unfortunately for the biker he struck the station wagon as it came through the green light. When he hit the car, the javelin ornaments stuck him between the eyes killing him instantly. There was a moment of silence and contemplation in the briefing room when the sergeant read this one.

Choices have consequences.

Part Four:

Do the Minimum get the Maximum

Chapter 14

300 ft. of old fence

A fully equipped police officer, 6' 5', in good shape, may weigh 250 lbs. in full gear. A pencil neck geek perpetrator about 5' 6' may weigh about 110 lbs. The perpetrator running through the back yards of a Highlands neighborhood encountering a 300 foot stretch of fence simply grabbed the top of the fence and leaped over. The 250 lb. patrolman right on his heals hits the same fence, and Bang! The whole 300 foot section of fence hits the ground. "Yikes! Yells the perp, as he hits the ground right after the fence. "Yikes!" yells the sergeant when he comes to inspect the fence. "Yikes!" yells the lieutenant reading the report. "Yikes!" yells the chief when he gets the bill for the fence.

(Note to reader the use of the word "Yikes is an attempt by the writer to clean up the language so you would not think ill of public officials)

In my defense, I pointed out to the chief that every post on that fence was rotted and a strong wind would have knocked it over. "Why does this crap always happen to you?" "Well chief, there are two philosophies around here. One is "work hard and your diligence will pay off." The other is "do the minimum, get the maximum."

(Note to reader: This is government. Which philosophy wins out in the end? It's the latter.)

This was never so true to me when one evening I responded to a domestic in the city. My back up was the Corporal. The Corporal and I were on the Sergeant's list. He was a "do the minimum" guy.

The older son of this family, The Perp we will call him, was a pain in the butt. He loved to assault family members. He was also aware of the implications of the new domestic violence act. He would have to go to jail. When we arrived The Perp skipped out the back into the woods. The Corporal showed up and quickly used the fact that The Perp was on the run to turn the report over to me while the Corporal went to look for The Perp. I took the information for my report from the mother and brother of The Perp.

I was sitting in the driveway of the residence doing the report when I was contacted by his brother. He told me that The Perp had returned to the residence and was again threating the mother. I informed Control that the situation was escalating. I requested my backup return.

I started for the front door. As I arrived at the door, I was immediately confronted by the mother, who ducked under my outstretched arm, which I had used to push open the door. She says as she goes past, "He was back and he has a gun." I had a clear view from the front door to the kitchen. As she went by, I saw The Perp appear from in front of the refrigerator. He had a 30/30 Winchester at port arms. Now, I am not about to turn my back on a guy with a 30/30. I don't care about the "S W A T needed to be involved B.S." the Chief with 20/20 hindsight wanted.

I drew my service weapon. I told him to drop the rifle and put his hands up. He began to advance towards me slowly with the weapon at port arms. I told him if that weapon started to move in my direction I would shoot him. He kept coming, telling me to leave. He walked right up to me. When he got close, I grabbed his rifle, and pushed him back over a glass topped table, smashing the table.

I fought the weapon away from him and threw it behind the couch. I was able to pin him on the floor and reach for my radio. I called, "OFFICER NEEDS HELP!" and continued the fight. I could hear the guys acknowledging, and giving their response times. A short time later the other district car showed up and we cuffed The Perp.

The Corporal, who was supposed to have been my backup, arrived several minutes later. We took the rifle and Perp to jail. The mom returned very upset that I had broken the coffee table, even scolding me saying we were going to pay for the table. The Chief at this time was a good administrator, but a lousy cop, a real "do the minimum" guy. The mayor was in love with him. She hired him over a real cop that the guild wanted. But that's another story.

The next day, I was called into the Chief's office. I was given a letter of reprimand. The letter was supported by a report from the Corporal. The Corporal postulated that I should have left the mom in the house and S.W.A.T. should have been called out to deal with the armed suspect. At this point, the Chief and I became less than tolerant with each other. I told him that I would keep his letter of reprimand next to my heart, and shoved it in my back pocket. The Corporal made Sergeant.

I never took another exam. I thought long and hard about leaving the department. In retrospect I wish I had. I later went to the Detective division and tried to bury myself in my work. The Chief and his political stooges were destined to screw up a few more cases before it was over.

During one homicide investigation I told him that he needed to bring in the state crime lab to go over the house, because we did not have the equipment, or the expertise, to gather the kind of trace evidence that would be needed to solve the case. The Chief refused and then let the press into the crime scene before we were ready.

At the shooting of one of our officers, at an office building, the Chief let the Mayor and his cronies walk around inside an active crime scene. Our major crimes guy and I had been called in from checking out a pile of deer bones, to this shooting. Our officer had been hit in the vest and was thankfully just bruised up a bit.

Press helicopters were circling the scene, and officers from a neighboring city were all over the place marking evidence. The new Mayor, the Chief, and the Capitan were running around inside the scene screwing things up. My partner and I assessed the situation. We saw the Mayor standing next to the suspect's weapon, all by himself. He was nervously playing with his tie and moving his foot, like he was thinking about kicking the weapon. He started to bend over to touch it when my partner and I intervened. "Mr. Mayor," I said, "you should not be here. There is press all over the place, and if they photograph you touching that weapon, I think your political career will be over." We then went to the Captain, and told him what was going on. He got the Chief and his stooges out of there.

MESSAGE TO ALL WOULD-BE POLICE CHIEFS: If you don't have major crime scene experience don't apply or stay away from crime scenes altogether.

If you find a guy with "do the minimum, get the maximum" ideas get the fool rid of him. Don't promote him.

When a traumatic situation occurs within a family group like the police, there is a tendency for the excitable elements among the family to lose perspective. When the members of the group that tend to lose perspective are command staff and politicians, the end result can be devastating. When you break it down, it is usually because they are more concerned with getting their pictures taken than completing the mission.

A day in the life of the Corporal

I was minding my own business on a warm fall day. Our Corporal had been dispatched to the scene of a car-deer encounter. The Corporal was one of those tender-hearted souls who had a hard time with gun play. He had been involved early in his career in a shootout with a robbery suspect in which his training officer was wounded.

After I cleared a call, the Corporal called me to assist him. I pulled up and the conversation went like this.

"Hi Knocker, I have situation here. There is this deer, and it has been hit by a car, and there is no animal control unit on duty now, and I was thinking you're good at this sort of thing. I just can't do it." "What am I good at?" I asked. "Well you know the deer is hurt? It keeps looking at me. I just can't do it, do you mind?"

I know you're thinking Officer Knocker was screwing with the Corporal, and you would be right. I was playing stupid with him, letting him dangle. He was a corporal and could order me to shoot the deer, but he could not bring himself to shoot the deer or to order me to do it. I am of the belief that if you are confronted with a situation like this and you don't take the opportunity to screw with the "do the minimum" office poge, you are just not being reasonable.

You have to have fun with this job or drink heavily. I chose fun. I kept obfuscating until he walked me over to the deer. I looked at it and said," Yeah, you should just shoot it when there are no cars in view." "Well a I well I can't a would you mind a." "Oh! Do you want me to shoot the thing?" I asked. "Well, yeah!" came the somewhat annoyed response. "Oh, ok." I said.

All the pent up tension that the Corporal was experiencing was released at that moment.

I pulled my weapon and fired one round hitting the deer between the eyes and re-holstered. The Corporal jumped straight up in the air and yelled, Dang it, Knocker! You were supposed to wait till I was ready." All the tension that was previously released was back. "You can't do this to me Knocker." "Why not? Isn't that why they pay you all that extra money? Do you want me to leave a note for animal control, or do you think you could do that? Yah I can do that. Oh I'll need a round to replace the one I fired? Here take one of mine says the corporal. Gee did you have to do that he asked? Well I'm off. See you later I said.

Chapter 15

Working Homicide

Unsolved homicides

Nothing in police work is more distasteful than to end your career with an unsolved homicide on the books. The definition of solved is this: we know or have a good idea who did it. In my career there are two cases that I was personally involved with that fit the definition. We had a good idea who did it. We were not able to make an arrest in the case of the Mexican kid, due to the unwillingness of the prosecutor to issue an arrest warrant because we had "not interviewed the suspect," never mind that he had fled to Alaska and was rumored to have been holed up in a small fishing village.

We were told that we could arrest him on an old traffic warrant if we could get the State of Alaska to extradite him on the warrant. Good luck with that. The victim was a local kid who had a drug and alcohol problem. He was found dead in the alley behind a local bar by one of our officers on patrol. An 80 pound rock had been dropped on his head. He was involved in a fight in a local bar and it had moved to the alley.

The kid had no identification on him at the time. We did not recognize him. The damage to his head had distorted his appearance. There was a sort of familiar sneer of his lips that I could not quite place. I knew that I had seen him before. We went to the autopsy. The doctor informed us the man was both a heavy drinker and marijuana user.

This was the key information needed for the identification; the sneer on his lips, and the heavy marijuana and alcohol use. I blurted out, "This is The Mexican Kid!" I asked the doctor how he knew the kid drank and was a marijuana user. He explained that alcohol causes the body to smell rank when cut open. We had noted this at the beginning of the autopsy. Heavy marijuana causes the liver to appear whitish in a star-like pattern when dissected. This is liver damage and it is made worse by the use of alcohol.

Isn't it just great that states are legalizing marijuana? Now our children can be driven in even greater numbers and faster into the clutches of those who would seek to do them harm. The perverts are licking their chops at the prospect of using this powerful new tool.

No matter though, we can tax the dope and use the revenue for the benefit of the teachers' union. Oh Goody, Goody, Goody! Remember: *Choices have consequences.*

The girl in the swamp was a bit different. We first got wind that there may be a problem when pieces of a skeleton started turning up in this isolated corner of our city. After an extensive search the source of the bones was located.

She had been stripped naked and dumped in a swamp. The swamp had dried up due to a drought that year, and the bones of a 14 year old alleged runaway were exposed at long last to wild animals that proceeded to scatter them about.

Our investigation led us to the house in the county where she had lived with her mom and stepdad. They had since moved but we got the permission of the landlord to search the house. The search turned up a suspicious area under a carpet that looked like blood had been cleaned up. The mother and stepdad were completely disinterested in the investigation.

She had been reported missing around the time of her death but that's as far as mom went. She just cleaned up the house and moved.

The teacher was the real regret. A murder without reason, a violent crime scene without significant evidence, and a bungling police chief who refused to understand the situation led to a Big Fat Zero.

The call came in as a violent home invasion. The phone wires had been cut, the back door entered, and the retired teacher stabbed to death in front of his legally blind wife. The responding officer nearly ran over the suspect leaving the scene. The only real description of the suspect was a tall dark shape.

I got the impression we were looking for a ninja or some kind of professional killer. Nothing in the victim's background seemed to warrant a professional hit. I was assigned to the crime scene, but with so little to go on and the Chief's unwillingness to call in the state crime lab, I felt it was unlikely to go anywhere and I was right. *Choices have consequences.*

Solved homicides: The girl and a roofing hammer,

On a warm afternoon in the late 80s my partner I were sent to a suspicious death at a small apartment complex in the city. It was a single story 8 unit complex with a laundry room in the center. The victim's apartment was located at the southeast corner of the complex. The victim was a middle aged white male about 5' 10" 150 lbs. He was lying on his bed on his back. He was dressed in the uniform of a security guard.

There were several square contusions on his forehead as though someone had sat on his chest and hit him with a hammer. Blood spatter on the walls and the blood trail showed the attack was violent and sustained.

When we arrived we noticed a female tenant washing clothing in the laundry. She had used too much soap and the suds were overflowing the machine. We interviewed this subject. She was a single mother with a 4 year old son. She had been the last person to see the victim the night before. She said she occasionally dated the victim. He had loaned her money in the past. We learned from others the victim had complained that he felt she was sneaking into his apartment at night and taking money from his wallet.

The blood trail from the victim's apartment led out the front door down the side walk past the laundry room and stopped in the area of the woman's apartment. We completed our work at the scene.

The next day we attended the autopsy. The wounds were examined and found to be the cause of death. The probable weapon was determined to be a roofing hammer with a square dimpling dead head about one inch square. We obtained a search warrant for the suspect's apartment. The woman and her 4 year old son were present during the search. We were looking for the hammer and any bloody clothing. I was standing next to the door while my partner conducted the interview with the woman.

While standing by the door I noticed hammer marks on the door casing that appeared to be similar to the dimpling on the skin of our victim. I brought this to my partner's attention. We took the molding as evidence and asked her where the hammer was. She denied having a hammer.

The 4 year old then said it is under the sink and went to the sink and looked. Mom's face got beet red. The boy turned to his mom and said the hammer was gone. It was at this point mom realized she was in big trouble and requested her lawyer. The crime lab made an exact match between the marks on the molding and the marks on the victim's head. She eventually pled guilty to murder. She gave an account of what had transpired.

The victim had caught her in the act of taking money from his wallet and started after her. She hit him with the hammer she brought with her for protection. He went down on the bed and was only stunned. He kept trying to get up and she kept hitting him until he quit moving. She had only intended to knock him out but he just didn't go out. This was affirmed by the medical examiner's note in his report. The victim had an extra heavy lining in his skull. This genetic condition would make him hard to knock out.

The gun shop shooting

It was the night of the Police Guild dinner dance. I was working in the detective division. I was called out to a shooting at local gun shop. A county deputy was involved. The scene was a mess. There was one D.O.A. shooter lying in a pool of his own blood, one shook up Deputy, one marked patrol car parked at the front door, a 9 mm on the floor next to the shooter. 9 and 10 mm casings were everywhere. There were holes all around where the officer and a store employee were standing.

It was one of those worst cases of suicide I'd ever seen.

The action started when the Deputy decided to stop and see his friends at the gun shop. He was in the store standing at the end of the counter facing the main door, talking with the elderly employee. A little chit chat about their favorite subject, guns and ammo.

(The Victim / Suspect / Shooter whatever you want to call him.)

(The real Victim of an unprovoked 1st degree assault and attempted murder was the County Deputy.)

The shooter pulled into the parking lot of the gun shop. He exited his vehicle, walked toward the main doors, and squeezed past the marked patrol car that the deputy had parked close to the building. After negotiating this obstacle, he entered the store by the main door. About 5 feet inside the store, the shooter pulls his 9 mm and commences firing on the Deputy.

The deputy pulls his 9 mm Glock and fires once. The weapon recoils and catches his thumb nail in the slide and jams. His fight is over. The employee sees the situation unfolding and takes action. Strapped on his hip is a loaded 10 mm Smith & Wesson. The employee gets off several rounds. All hit their mark and the shooter is down. In all, about 18 rounds were fired, but the shooter was the only one hit. When the body was removed by the coroner, several 50 cent size disks fell to the floor. These were determined to be slugs from the employee's 10 mm Smith & Wesson.

The crime scene team and I spent the rest of the evening trying to find all the holes in the wall the shooter made. We found all but two that night. The next day, a King County team went in and removed all the peg board in the shop and found the other two holes.

I had already cleared the case as the attempted murder of a deputy and a self-defense killing of a deranged citizen. I sent it to my lieutenant for his approval. Case closed.

Part Four:

The effects of the
drug culture

Chapter 16

Druggies

In the late 90s, several years before I retired, I got a call in an apartment complex off N.E. 4th. A suspect was being tracked by the dog handler in the woods east of the apartments. This dog had never found anyone while I was around. Several of us were saying the dog was just a pet. It couldn't track a cat and couldn't even track a bitch in heat. You know the comments. . . good natured but hurtful things.

This day the dog must have been feeling good because we kept hearing the dog barking, growling and generally hostile sounds in the woods. I was on the west side of the woods looking up hill over a rockery when everything went quiet. I was just about to ask what was happening when I hear rustling in the bush right above me. Then there was an explosion of fur, blood and mankind rolling out of the blackberries. The dog had this guy in a rolling mass of fur and blood and drenched clothing. They were hung up in the blackberries. Right above me I reached out and grabbed the suspect by the hair and jerked him loose.

As soon as I had him the dog quit and let go. "Good boy!" I told the dog. I told the suspect to lie still until the dog handler could get the dog. He happily complied. I had blood all over me. When the dog man arrived, I asked him about the suspect. A few weeks earlier this burglar had been arrested after falling from a third story window in an attempt to burglarize a third floor apartment. He tells me that the guy is a hype and is rumored to have H.I.V. Now we are all going to the hospital for an H.I.V. test. We test him and we're relieved that he is negative.

Here is a real problem in police work. The idea that every criminal is entitled to bail needs to be reexamined. This guy was a serial offender he was a known user of narcotics. There was no way a reasonable person would think that he was not going to go right back to his criminal ways. He had a drug problem that rendered him unemployable. The only way to get the money he needed to get his fix was to steal. Let's call it what it is levying another tax on victims.

Let's be 10% smarter than these tortured souls. Make their drugs free, and give them a place to go and use them. Let's give them a reservation, in every state, where they can be kept, and give the crime victim a break. Why do we levy this tax on victims, in the name of criminal justice? Stop treating it as a crime per se. Treat it as a public health issue that requires quarantine of the individual. A free drug for the addicts is a tax I would rather pay than the tax to lock them up for their criminal acts.

What do we get for this?

1   It will take all the incentive for drug dealers to produce drugs and infect new users. We could just take the drugs from them and give the drugs to the addict ourselves. As time passes there will naturally be fewer and fewer addicts to supply.
2   We would have a 50% reduction in crime overnight.
3   Death on our highways will be reduced.
4   Police will be able to redirect to other threats.
5   The end result should be lower taxes.

My idea then is to create a reservation system in each state where they could do all the drugs they want for free, as long as they last. We take the drugs away from the suppliers and ship them to the reservations where they can be used. The druggies would be civilly quarantined until they go through a rehab or die. It is the nuclear option. Let the churches, families, and any groups that want to save them have free access to them, but the druggy can't leave till he or she takes the cure. Every user goes, there are no exceptions.

There would be no incentive to sell, as the seller and his clients would be sent to the reservation. Most crime would end. The spread of this scourge would largely stop. All the do-gooders would have access to them and could encourage them to get straight. The hooked ones would have all they wanted. Everybody wins. We could save billions for social programs. Cops could concentrate on real crime.

The marijuana plant

I guess it was in the late 70's. There are those that say I should know that date like it was yesterday, and for a while I certainly did. Frankly, in my old age, dates and feelings of remorse have begun to fade.

I had started swing shift with a domestic call at a house. The house was one of those two bedroom WWII homes and was used as a rental. The renter and her boyfriend were a couple of hippies.

Peace and love were not working for them that day. When I got to the call, the boyfriend had left the scene. I talked to the young lady. She was not saying she had been assaulted, just that they had been arguing, and she wanted to be left alone. I was trying to be sympathetic. I assured her that everything would work out, they just needed time.

It was a warm day in mid-summer. They had started a small garden. I had noticed this when I arrived. I suggested that she do some gardening, and take her mind off the disagreement. She thought that might be a good Idea. As we walked out of the house, I took a good look at the garden. There between two tomato plants was a well-tended marijuana plant.

If I had known, how this day would have ended, for this family, I would have just left and let them do their thing. This one case has probably formed my thinking as to what to do about the drug problem in America more than anything else I can think of. It consumed my thinking and my approach to police work. The little things that police officers do can have far reaching and devastating effects on individuals. I could rationalize that I was not responsible for what she did as a result of my decision not to arrest her and her boyfriend for growing marijuana. How could I know the devastating effect my decision would have on her?

After spotting the marijuana in the garden, I said to her, "You know that growing marijuana is a felony." She said, "It's my baby," as she broke out in tears. I should have arrested her at this point, but I didn't. I just pulled up the plant, chucked it in my trunk, and gave her a warning. I transported the plant to the station for disposal.

About two hours later, the boyfriend returned to the house. He found the young lady lying on the bed with a 22 cal. bullet through her head. There was a note stating she just couldn't take it anymore. The boyfriend felt it was his fault. I felt it was my fault. She died at Valley General Hospital and the detectives and I cleaned up the mess.

It is no wonder that I would take the position that we should do away with criminal arrests for drug violations, and just give the druggies a place to do all the drugs they want for free. If we did this it would remove the incentive to sell drugs, and stop the spread of them. *Choices have consequences.*

Now I have explained the situation and articulated a cure. It is a win, win, win. What more could you all want

It is like the River City Loop. We just need to make doing drugs illegal and mean it. It all boils down to the theory that in order to stop a person from doing things that are destructive to civil order we have to give them a reason not to do the act in question.

The bikers at Misty Cove

I am going to start this explanation of an aspect of human conduct with a bit of history as it regards the formation of some of these biker gangs.

In every major war that this nation has engaged in, the aftermath has spawned disaffected groups of mostly veterans that turn somewhat lawless. The probable cause of this is the malady known today as P T S D. We send soldiers off to fight. We pin medals on them for doing things that in civilized society they would be hanged for doing. The war ends and they are all sent home.

Going home physically does not mean that you are home mentally. I know this because when I came back from Korea in 1966 after spending 9 months along the DMZ and enduring the stress of that deployment, I was just a bit jumpy.

I had no more gotten off the plane at Travis Air Force Base in California when we were confronted by a bunch of leftwing protesters jeering and spitting on us. We asked the Lieutenant who was marching us to the processing center if we could fall out and take on that crowd of hippie assholes. They can thank their lucky stars that permission was denied.

When I arrived home, I was still in war mode. I came in the house and greeted my parents. My younger brother made the mistake of thinking I was the same old big brother he could spar with when I left. The first thing he did was to give me a big howdy and faint a punch to my head. He was playing but I reacted before I could think. I had hit him and spun him around knocking one of his teeth out in the process.

My dad, a W W ll veteran, saw the whole thing and jumped in. I was apologizing to him when dad lit in to him. Dad told him and the others that you can't do that to any soldier coming back from a war zone. I spent the rest of the day trying to make it up to my brother and dad.

As a whole, my P T S D was minor. I was deployed to a relatively quiet area. There were only a few major alerts where we were locked and loaded.

Imagine the intensity of P T S D when it involves actual war. Friends are killed. You are fighting for your life. The transition back to the real world may be slow if it comes at all. Those that can't or refuse to adjust tend to gather together and continue the war at home, drinking and fighting. They can't work so they take up criminal pursuits.

Motorcycle gangs were formed out of this malaise. The gangs themselves are basically super patriotic and loosely militaristic organizations. They have a rank structure and have their own colors (symbols of their units) that they may be willing to die for. It is the camaraderie of the military without the discipline. This can be very attractive to a segment of this population of veterans, and some non-veterans raised in chaotic homes.

Policing these folk is an art. They must be respected and allowed to exist while enforcing the discipline of society in a way that is acceptable to them and societal norms. This usually means that the police will have to show force, and then make a peace treaty acceptable to all.

We accomplished this balance in River City in the 1980s by making a chippie arrest of one of the members. We booked the individual, and then washed his colors, (the vest he wore with the gang insignia). This vest is given when a member is voted in to the gang and is never to be washed. After we washed the colors, they sued for peace, our conditions were met and they were allowed to exist.

Prior to this incident, we had a large gathering of bikers in the area of north River City. They were confrontational and doing drugs openly. We arrested a dealer out of the gathering and booked him. To avoid an open war, we backed off, telling them we would deal with them as individuals. When a few started to leave, we made arrests. It was just enough to make our point.

At the hearing of the drug dealer, the district court judge put me on the stand. I was a new officer and it was my first time in his court. The judge was looking to see if we had probable cause for the arrest. I was testifying that I had seen this individual wearing a top hat dispensing reds out of the hat.

Reds were the street name for a barbiturate circulating at that time. I took my shot gun and snuck up on the gathering while other officers engaged the main body. The dealer was sneaking around a bush. I caught him dumping the drugs. I stuck the shotgun in his face and arrested him. As soon as I said "I arrested him" the judge stopped me. He leaned over his desk and said to the dealer, "You were selling those drugs, weren't you!?" before his attorney could object, the dealer says, "yes, your honor". With that the judge jumps out of his chair, slams his gavel down, and yells, "BOUND OVER!" I nearly jumped out of my chair when he did that

Hippies at the Bronson Texaco

It was a swing shift. My partner and I were working the downtown cars. At briefing we had been asked by the narcotics division to be on the lookout for a couple of notorious brothers who had drug warrants out for them.

We had gotten out of our cars at about 17:30. The sun was going down. We were walking on S Third. We observed the suspect we had been asked to look out for traveling eastbound on S Third in a yellow Cadillac.

We ran up jumped in a taxi cab, which was passing. We told the driver to follow the car. To our delight, the driver cooperated and we followed the car down across the bridge and along the railroad track. As the car approached the intersection, a train coming southbound on the tracks blocked the vehicles from turning east. The driver aborted the attempt, turning the car sharply and then killing the engine. The vehicle rolled into The Texaco station.

At this point, responding officers pulled into the lot. The vehicle was full of drugged out hippies. As my partner and I pulled up behind the car, there were about a dozen individuals stumbling around in the lot attempting to avoid the officers who were trying to take them into custody.

One of the individuals who had the felony warrant was standing in the middle of the lot at the Texaco with people running all around. My partner and I watched as this individual, apparently feeling that no one had seen him, started a high-stepping tippy toe walk as though he were in a cartoon attempting to avoid Wile E. Coyote. He tiptoed this way with his head going back and forth as though he were looking for somewhere to go.

He tiptoed right past us across the street to the park which was located just south of the Texaco. He then tiptoed over to a hedge next to the pool. He parted the hedge with his hands. Looking left then right he stepped over the hedge, turned around, and sank down next to the fence.

My partner and I strolled over to the hedge in a nonchalant fashion. When we got over to the hedge, we reached over, each of us grabbing an arm and jerked him back out over the hedge and arrested him. He was booked on the felony narcotics warrants.

He was on those so called "mind expanding drugs"

A van full of hippies, a street full of reds, all the little children bounced on their heads

I was working the 2 Robert 9 district. I spotted one of those VW vans that were popular with hippies back in the 70s. The van was headed eastbound on NE 12th. It was full of hippy wanna-bes. I turned in behind the vehicle and began following the thing. As the van traveled eastbound on NE 12th, it was weaving all over the road. I called for backup. We had a unit coming to assist from N.E. 4th. As we proceeded east on 12th the driver must have spotted me as the vehicle accelerated and turned south. This put the van between me and the responding back up unit.

The hippies were now in a fix, pretty lights behind and pretty lights coming from the front.

A popular theme of the Drug culture was that L.S.D. and Marijuana were "Mind Expanding Drugs." It just isn't so folks. If they were, these whack jobs would have felt an overwhelming impulse to stop back at the library on N.E. 12th and I never would have gotten involved in their little social experiment.

As the van approached N.E. 10th Pl. the realization of their impending doom and the paranoia that so often accompanies the ingestion of certain of these mind altering substances kicked in.

All these events happened at once. The van stopped, I blocked the rear escape route, the responding car blocked the van from the front, the side door on the van opened, and out on their heads rolled seven hippies, with a cloud of marijuana smoke enveloping the entire scene. As one of the participants hit the street he dropped the bag of reds he was holding. (*Reds are the street name for a barbiturate popular at the time*) The reds went all over the street. The stunned and panicked hippies were laying everywhere, some with their legs still in the van. At about this time several other units arrived to partake in the fun of corralling this group of drugged out friends of Dr. O'Leary.

At this time in my career, I had made a number of these types of arrests. Some of the older officers were remarking and questioning how, I, a mere rookie, was able to, "slop into all these major arrests." The answer was that I didn't subscribe to the notion that I should "do the minimum and get the maximum." It was good police work. I wasn't out stopping every blonde chick I saw driving a hot car. That is <u>exactly</u> what a large numbers of the lamenters were doing with their time.

A second reason was: I was raised in a poor section of the city I grew up in. I had experience with a lot of these criminal elements, and I could read them like a book.

The down side was that the more arrests of this nature you made the more the criminal public complained. If we had a good chief, this was not a problem, as long as the arrests were legal and justified. When we got a chief that was more of a politician than a real cop, he didn't like the fact that you got a citizen's complaint at all.

The "Do the Minimum and Get the Maximum" guys won the top administrative jobs. That eventually led to the internet puppet show years after I retired. To me it was the right on and was the funniest thing I had ever scene. See you tube cyberstalking cartoons 1 through 9

Are the people of River City getting the type of policing they deserve? Maybe! What I do know is the people in any governmental agency who subscribe to the "Do the Minimum and Get the Maximum" philosophy are thieves taking a paycheck for doing a job they have no intention of doing well.

The solution lies with the voters. Unfortunately for the nation, the voters are being dumbed down by an education system that is top-heavy with liberalism.

Until balance is restored in education, the slide into ignorance will continue. An uneducated, ignorant electorate is easy to control with accusations of prejudice.

This seems to me to be what the liberals are striving for. Why else would they fight to keep criminals from being fired for offenses involving children? Why do so-called rubber rooms exist in some school systems? Why are liberal professors inciting students to chase conservative speakers from campuses all across this nation? Why are collage kids out in the streets fighting with police when they should be in class learning how to, learn and to think before they try to speak?

Part Five:

Defining Stupid

Chapter 17

10% smarter than the thing you are trying to control

There are people of great intelligence who are dumb as a post when it comes to the control of human conduct.

Simple problems simple solutions: usually one needs to be just 10% smarter than the thing you are trying to control. This is true in most of man's endeavors. I cannot understand how it is that given this maxim, why a grown adult cannot control a two year old.

I believe it is because they are over-thinking the problem and seeking advice from experts when the solution lies at the end of your arm. The hand is a marvelous instrument. The hand can grip things, it can scratch your butt, perform wondrous works of art, or even surgery. But its highest calling is the control of the toddlers that infest our lives and either bring great joy or misery on a case-by-case basis.

To quote Jase Robertson, "Just because you're smart don't mean you're smart." Abe Lincoln said, "People are just about as happy as they make up their minds to be." In my house children are not allowed to be unhappy. My grandfather was fond of saying, "be happy or I will give you a reason to be unhappy." Thank God I always instinctively knew the meaning of that statement.

This wisdom was generational in our family. Great Grandpa was a Methodist minister. Being happy and forgiveness were not optional. They are bedrock concepts. They are instilled in the toddler from the first breath to out of the house!

Beyond the grave for that matter: my father rarely said anything except, "if grandpa has to spank you I'm going to swat you too." Grandpa was always saying something, usually along the lines of, "if you do X you will cry before you go to bed." We all knew what that meant. Knock it off or I will swat you. The only time I can remember Grandpa carrying out the threat was when the three of us older boys went up to the lake without telling anyone. We got our butts kicked that day.

We knew we were going to "get it" when we got home. We stopped at the corner store, and begged some cardboard off the store owner. We stuck some down our pants. Then we eagerly confessed our transgression to Grandpa, when he asked, "just where have you boys been? Everyone is out looking for you boys." He was about to lay into us when he spotted the cardboard. Without a word he grabbed each of us in turn and booted us off the porch.

Then he said, "You know, I only have to be 10% smarter than you." Picking ourselves up from the middle of the back yard, we got the message. It never happened again. I am 68 years old now and I still miss the wisdom of my grandfathers. My kids think this stuff comes from me, but it doesn't, it was mostly passed down from them.

Most of the kids I encountered in police work came from families that either neglected the duty to discipline their children, or refused because they listened to a so-called expert on child rearing like Dr. Spock. These people have a monetary incentive to have as many screwed up kids in the general population as possible. Is it any wonder they advocate the things they do? They make money doing it, and fools like us go for it.

Grandpa said, "If a child is fussy and is not sick, he is tired, hungry or his shoes are too tight. Eliminate these. Take off their shoes, feed them, and its nap time. Peace will return to the house, when we get up from our naps.

HOW to Discipline Children?

Children are our most prized possessions. They are gifts from God. Think of your children this way: they are more valuable than your Rolex watch. You would not give your Rolex to the guy down the street to look at, let alone play with for the day. You keep it on the end of your arm. You put it in a safe place at night. If you want to store it, you put it in the bank storage box with a banker you trust. Disciplining children is like keeping the watch band tight so it doesn't fall off your arm.

1 Recognize that the day a child is born, they are trying to discipline you! You should not allow yourself to become the victim here.

2 They are hard wired to get your attention. You must submit to their needs. You are hard wired to do just that. Don't give in to the notion that every whimper needs some hands-on attention. Be vigilant but smart; they are working you.

3 Now you watch them carefully. When they start making you do things that are not necessary for life to be sustained, like the "pick me up and walk the floor with me" game, start your own counter actions. Frown at them, and tell them you are wise to this game. Do all the preventive maintenance things: check the diapers, feed and burp them, give them the "you're not fooling me speech," everything but what they want.

4 As they get older they are looking for a smile from you, give it when they are doing well, and frown and tell them you

don't like it when they are not with the program. It won't take long and they will respond to your smiles and frowns. If their diaper is dry, remember the axiom, if they are fussy, they are hungry, tired, or their shoes are too tight.

Diapers are meant to be changed regularly. We used the cloth type. The boys had rubber pants for some protection against accidents. One day when the twins were about two, we went in to their room to check on them. They had cribs one on each side of the room. When we got in the room, there they were both sporting their rubber pants on their heads. Of course I took a picture of this mile stone of their development. I will never forget how perfectly proud of themselves they were.

5 As they get older they begin to respond to voice, use your happy voice and your unhappy voice.

6 Older yet, about 6 to 18 months, or when they take their first steps, go to the paint department of the local hardware store and get two large paint sticks and some duct tape. Wrap one stick handle until there is a wad of tape on one stick. Place the other stick on the top of the duct tape and wrap both sticks together this should give you a stick with ½ inch of separation at the other end. After the handle is wrapped, slap the sticks across your knee. You should here a sharp crack.

For those of you who need the designer this or that, I have a line of designer paint sticks.

Toddlers are hard wired to show concern when they hear this sound. It gets there attention. If you pat them on the diaper with this, it really gets their attention. There is a button back there that is wired to the brain. It doesn't take much to activate it. Once you have activated the button it can be activated remotely by a sudden slap of the stick across your knee. Once you have activated this sequence, you are in control.

Don't let this new power go to your head; it can be over used. If you do use the stick it should followed up with hugs and a nap. When you get up from your naps, things should be back to normal.

7 There are those who will say this is mean and cruel. Answer this way: the cops are not going to be responsible to discipline my children. I will do it because I love them. I will not hurt them more than is necessary to fix the problem. I will teach my child that the parents are the only ones who have a right to discipline them. I will love them enough to do it well.

My wife is the master of this. Our boys walked quietly in a line behind her where ever we went. They took our hands when we reached out to guide them across a street or through some area that might be dangerous. In short, they were ours and they knew it. She rewarded them on most every trip with some small toy or a treat, their choice. If they misbehaved, no treat. Those days were rare in our house.

Around Christmas, she put up the treat tree. The boys had to make some ornament to go on the tree in order to get a daily treat. It never mattered what the ornament looked like or how old they got. They played along and got their treat. Once, the youngest boy could not think of a thing to make for the tree. Mom said a ball of tin foil would work. Bingo, he had his ornament.

When the boys got older and screwed up, I told them that if they wanted to be little criminals, I would have to train them for the only kind of work that I felt that they might get: ditch digging. I made them dig me a ditch. I always had a project in mind. I would wait until I caught one of them screwing up enough to warrant a ditch. I would always let it be known that I was thinking about some new project that required a ditch.

I got three ditches; the fourth learned from the mistakes of his brothers.

When they started to ride the bus to school I took them out and showed them how to cross the street. I told them that I was the only one that had the right to hurt them, and they were not allowed to get run over by cars. I said that I was watching, and if I did not see them stop and look both ways when crossing the street to the bus, and they didn't get hit by a car and get hurt, I would hurt them. On one occasion, the youngest twin failed to look crossing the street. All the other boys stopped and looked. He just walked out without looking.

When they came home, all the boys came in, and I walked over and punched the offender in the shoulder. "Ouch, what was that for?" he asked. I said, "You know the rule, you crossed the street and didn't look both ways. You didn't get hurt, so I get to hurt you." "Did that hurt?" I asked? "Yes!" "Good," I said.

Every day after that, he went to the edge of the road and stopped. His head went right, left and back at dad who was watching. All the boys got the message: they knew I cared about them.

Chapter 18

Something to think about

In the late 1980s, a young lady approximately 19 years old was booked into the River City jail on a prostitution charge and possession of narcotics.

She was in the jail approximately 2 weeks when she became ill. Her stomach began to swell; she had a fever, and was in great pain. Fire department medics were called in and they recommended she be rushed to the emergency room. After a careful examination by the emergency room staff, it was determined and that the young lady had neglected to remove a tampon from her last menstrual cycle. A raging infection had resulted from this lack of hygiene. No more boom, boom for this baby san.

This should make every John wonder just what they are "getting into".

Around the same time as the aforementioned hooker incident, I had an occasion to arrest a local bridge tramp, on a shoplifting charge. I brought the individual into the booking area and had him stripped-down to put him in jail coveralls. When the individual removed his shoes, I noted that his feet were wrapped in newspaper. The newspaper had been on his feet so long that it had embedded into his flesh. When questioned regarding the newspaper embedded into the flesh of his feet, his comment was that he had not had his shoes off in three months. It was the beginning of spring. He apparently wrapped his feet in newspaper at the start of winter, and did not remove the shoes the entire winter. He was transported to hospital and I never saw him again. I heard he lost his feet.

I suppose the moral to these stories are that hygiene is important for hookers, Johns and bridge tramps.

The Ozzy Osborne caper

The late 1970s and 80s was a drug sex and rock 'n roll era. I was a country and western fan; I didn't care much for the rock 'n roll scene. We had an influx of new officers during that time, and a number of them were heavy metal fans. They were always playing their music loud, even in the patrol cars when they're supposed to be listening for burglars. One of these officers was a particular fan of Ozzy Osborne. When we found out that Ozzy Osborne was going to come to one of our local stores, this officer was extremely excited and volunteered for crowd control at the event.

There were about six of us, including the chief of police. There was a short concert at the store. Ozzy Osborne was using the loading dock as a stage. A crowd of about 1,000 people were gathered in the parking lot. We had the area contained by a semicircle of officers in front of the crowd.

One of our officers was a huge fan. I will call the officer "the Fan." The Fan began circling back and forth in front of the band. It appeared as though he was in some distress. Several of us commented on his nervous demeanor. Just after the last set was played, the Fan started edging up to the stage area.

When Mr. Osborne stopped speaking to the crowd, the Fan suddenly rushed the stage. Grabbing his own shirt, he ripped it open, exposing his bulletproof vest to Mr. Osborne.

He then shouted, "Ozzy, sign my vest!" Ozzy didn't miss a beat. He just picked up the pen and in gold letters signed "Ozzy Osborne" across the Fan's vest.

I looked over at the chief of police, who was standing about 10 feet away from me, with his mouth dropped open. The crowd cheered, the chief looked around and decided not to call him on it at that time. The Fan was quickly ushered away to the station.

Later I had occasion to be walking down the hallway leading to the chief's office. The Fan was in the chief's office. The Chief was yelling at him. "You'd better never pull another stunt like that again." All the Fan could say was, "Chief, I couldn't help myself, he was my idol." The Fan came out of the chief's office red-faced and smiling. As he walked past me in the hallway, he looked up at me with a big smile and said, "the chief is going to let me keep the vest."

The Fan, in my opinion, would have made a better Wall Street banker than a cop. He was a guy everyone liked. I just would not have picked him for a partner. He was more the friend type.

Cop haters and mud puddles

In the late 1970s during the rainy fall we would occasionally get large puddles of water forming over clogged storm drains. During these times, I would carry a small rake in my patrol car so when I found one of these large puddles, I could get out of the patrol car just rake off any blocking debris. This usually cleared the puddle quickly and avoided me having to take an accident report.

Believe it or not, there are individuals whom we allow to drive automobiles who do not have enough sense to slow their vehicle down when going through these puddles. On one occasion, I spotted a large puddle blocking two lanes on Logan Avenue at Airport Way, near the high school stadium. I pulled my car up in the stadium parking lot. I got my rake out and walked over to the road's edge. I then put my hands up to stop traffic. I started to rake the leaves off the storm drain. One of the vehicles, a Jeep driven by one of our local female idiots, saw her chance. She was at the head of the line and presumably saw me bent over raking leaves off the drain. She gunned the engine and streaked towards me, washing me down. I immediately ran to my patrol car, jumped in and chased her down. I arrested her for reckless driving. She said she thought this incident was extremely funny, until she got before the judge.

After testifying as to what I had seen and what she had done, the local judge was not happy, giving her both a fine and jail time. This was unusual because he was one of our most liberal judges. This may have been because the judge felt I was acting outside the box of what he thought police officers do. 70% of a patrolman's time is spent doing things like clearing hazards, spotting street lights that are out, or talking to some kid on the corner about how the Seahawks are doing. It's called Public Service.

What do these last stories have in common? They are all acts related to self-discipline. The hooker is lazy and lacks the discipline to keep herself clean. The john cannot control his sexual urges and puts himself and others in danger of who knows what? The police officer can't conduct himself as a professional. The girl in the car lives in a world of hate. She can't control her burst of emotion because of her twisted view of the police and her desire for revenge. Because I knew this girl well I can say she was undisciplined as a child and was reflecting the views of parents that opted out in the struggle to raise the nation's youth.

Chapter 19

A study in diplomacy

Shortly after I joined the department in 1969, we became a mecca for outlaw motorcycle gangs. I had been on the department for approximately 2 months, when there was a large gathering of the Banditos motorcycle gang at the Cove Apartments. Approximately 300 bikers were in attendance.

We had received numerous complaints regarding noise and drug activity at this rally. We were outnumbered and the gang members were extremely bold and cantankerous. They refused to cooperate and were issuing verbal threats to take us out. A group of us were staked out observing this gathering in the Cove when I spotted an individual who appeared to be passing out drugs. He was wearing an old-fashioned top hat. He appeared to have the drugs inside the hat. After observing this I saw the individual disappear behind a hedge. I took my shotgun and I snuck up on the individual and arrested him with about 150 Reds in his possession. This arrest agitated the biker group, but we arrested the individual and then backed out of the area.

We warned them that when they tried to leave, they had better go quietly or we would start effecting arrest. Several hours later, some of the bikers started to leave the rally. Two of them went up onto the freeway and started riding in circles. They were blocking traffic. They got off their bikes and were cavorting with some of the female bikers, blocking the freeway. We arrested the small group of individuals. They were booked for disorderly conduct and a court date was set.

The judge who heard the case was our local police court judge. He was very liberal. He had a habit of finding ways to let these kinds of individuals off with little or no punishment. Small fines and suspended jail time were usually the order of the day.

On the day of the trial, these normally dirty, smelly, scruffy bikers came to court all cleaned up and in three-piece suits. We testified to the actions of these individuals and to the circumstances of their arrest. The judge listened quietly. He kept looking at these young men before him, and it was at this point that all of us got some insight into the thinking of our liberal judge.

Finding the individuals guilty of the acts, he made the following comments. "These young men I am looking at here appear to be well-mannered and well-educated. I could understand this kind of behavior from young men who obviously are not as privileged as these young men seem to be. I would be tempted to be lenient on young men who come from a background or an upbringing which fostered this kind of behavior. It's obvious to me that these young men were raised in privilege and understand right from wrong."

He threw the book at them, giving them fines and punishment hitherto unheard of in his court. From that point on, every time one of us arrested a biker, we told him to come to court a three-piece suit.

We played these games with bikers off and on over the next couple years. The bikers started hanging out at a tavern across from the airport on Airport Way. We begin to have fights, stabbings, and rowdy drunken behavior in and around the tavern. Adjacent businesses were beginning to complain that the situation was out of control. A new officer who had transferred from California was working with the squad at the time. Several of us went over to the tavern and attempted to reason with this group of Banditos.

After it became apparent they were not going to cooperate, we backed out and waited. Sure enough, a couple of them came out of the tavern carrying open bottles of beer in their hands and drinking. The Sergeant, the new guy, and I arrested the individuals for drinking in public. The new officer had recently joined the department, coming up from the department in southern California. The officer suggested that the way to handle these Banditos was simply to wash their colors.

We had never heard of this before. He explained that initiation into these motorcycle gangs requires that the individuals purchase a vest, with their appropriate patches on it. They then urinated on the vest, defecate and otherwise defile this article of clothing. The article of clothing is worn by the individuals and is never washed. To get your colors washed is a disgrace.

To those of us in the River City Police Department, particularly our squad, this was extremely interesting. We took the individual into the station booked him for drinking in public and slowed the booking process while we took him out of his clothing and put him into a jail jumpsuit.

Taking his clothing over to the laundry, we then ran his clothing through a cycle of the washing machine, pouring bleach all over it. About the time we had run the clothing through the washer, the individuals from the tavern showed up to make his bail. We then threw the individual's clothing in the dryer and turned the dryer on. It took us about an hour to process the individual out of jail because, as we later told the captain, we were rather busy.

As soon as the items were dried, the Sergeant went to his locker and retrieved a bottle of Brute cologne. We sprinkled all the clothing with Brute. We took the clothing and set it in the booking office. All the time that this individual was being processed out of the police department, we were bantering back and forth with him kind of "yakking it up" as we say, in an attempt to foster a little levity.

The last thing we did was slide his clothing over to him and tell him to get dressed. He took one look at the clothing and his mouth dropped open. He grabbed it and threw it on the floor. He started screaming, "You don't know what you've done!" We told him, "oh yes we do know what we've done, and if you guys want to keep giving us a hard time on the street, this is what's going to happen every time one of you comes in here." With this he got dressed and was taken out to his cronies who were waiting in the lobby. They stormed out of the police department and we all went about our business.

The next day, the assistant chief came to our briefing and informed us he had been contacted by representatives of the biker gang. They were requesting a truce. He then told us there would be no more washing of colors by the River City Police Department. We told the Chief to impart to the individuals that we would not wash their colors if they did not break the truce. That was the end of problems with motorcycle gangs in River City.

Lesson: speak softly and carry a bottle of Brute.

A liberal judge takes the cure

The District Court was a fairly decent district court. The judges were knowledgeable and, for the most part, we had very few problems with the judges. However, one judge was something of a liberal and seemed to go out of his way to make it hard for us to obtain search warrants. He tended toward leniency for many of the miscreants we would bring before him.

You have to understand that police officers do not just go out and arrest people because they like to. The paperwork involved is horrendous. If you screw up enough to get arrested and booked into jail, there's a pretty good likelihood that you deserve everything you are going to get.

After several years of dealing off and on with this particular judge who shall remain nameless, he went back to a meeting on the east coast for judges. During the time he was there, he got himself mugged and landed in the hospital for quite some time. When he returned to us, it seemed that he was a changed man. Search warrants were easier to obtain. If something wasn't right in the affidavit, he helped us make it right. He gave us advice on how better to proceed, and was available pretty much whenever we needed.

After witnessing this transformation, I concluded that it might be a good idea in the training of judges, if you could just take him back east and get them mugged. Maybe we wouldn't have problems with judges not understanding that police officers, for the most part, don't like paperwork. We only do it when we absolutely have to. You can take that to the bank. It doesn't fit in with their "Do the Minimum, Get the Maximum" credos.

Pastor John Hagee, my favorite pastor, gave a sermon based on David and Psalm 51. It was called "Guilty as charged." The theme of the dissertation was taking personal responsibility for the choices in our lives. The following is a quote from Pastor Hagee's sermon.

"All great living comes when we take personal responsibility for our transgression. It's not your mothers fault, not your father's fault, not the governments fault; it is your fault. You are responsible for your transgressions"

Choices have consequences and we all have to take responsibility for our actions.

I left the detective division late in my career. My duties included taking prisoners back and forth between the county jail and the city jail. I soon tired of the mouthy crap I would have to endure from the rear seat in the patrol car. I had been listening to the sermon series that the Pastor was preaching at the time. I took to carrying the tape of the sermon in my briefcase. I played it to drown out the guff from the back seat.

To my surprise, the sermon had a positive effect on the folks I was transporting. By the time I got to the jail, all was quiet. Some were crying, some thanked me, nobody complained. I thought sure that someone would make a formal complaint, but no one ever did. I transported hundreds before I retired. They all got to hear the tape. I still have it. I make all the grandkids listen to it whenever I can.

The A C L U will undoubtedly argue that this violated the rights of criminals sense they were at the time in a captive environment. Well Mr. A C L U attorney I have the right to listen to what I choose and hearing no objection from the rear seat, I guess I can choose to listen to whatever the hell I want to. All those other cops were listening to their tunes. I listen to mine, they got no complaints, and I got no complaints. If just one of these people started to take personal responsibility because of their exposure to that teaching, society will be better off. After all it is not about the government or religion; it is about civil society and personal responsibility.

Most of the sermons that are taught in churches of all faiths are secular and are not aimed at selling the religion. It is my experience that they are aimed taking responsibility for ones actions the Ten Commandments are for the most part aimed at maintaining a civil society. The argument is over who says we must obey the commandments. Those of us that believe give God the nod. The great I AM says we must obey. The non-believer says the government is the ultimate authority under the heavens. We all, that is all civilized people agree there has to be rules and the rules must be followed or civilization breaks down.

In a sense we are arguing over whom or what is GOD The secularists say the government is the ultimate authority and in the case of democracy the people are GOD. Those of us that choose to believe in our GOD, believe that there is an ultimate authority. We the people are individually responsible to him. He has given us commandments to follow as we establish governance over our fellow man.

Chapter 20

The track

The local horse track had 7 or 8 bars and numerous concessions. There was a large two-story kitchen complex that served the track. There were several cupolas overlooking the grandstand. Behind the main betting lines there was a money room. All these places had a check station where the night watchman would come to key his time clock.

There was a night watchman, an old civilian who made regular rounds with the clock. The armed guards also made random rounds with a clock. The guards also wandered at large. All together, the place was pretty secure. One night a week during the season, we stood by with heavy weapons while the weekly count was made and money was transfer to an armored car.

We all carried radios, even the old night watchman. He was a nice old guy, but he had trouble understanding how to work a hand-held radio. Most every time he called, he forgot to let go of the button, and had to be reinstructed daily on radio procedure. One day I sat him down in the office. I tried to show him the "Army way." Since he was checking bars, I gave him the handle "Heated Bar Fly." I was "Heated Bar Fly Echo."

At that time, we had front side guards and back side guards. I informed the back side that I was re-training the night watchman on radio procedure. They were glad of this, as the watchman was always stepping on their transmissions.

After about an hour of testing the watchman on the radio, it seemed that he had the idea. Out he goes too station one. "Heated Bar Fly Echo, this is Heated Bar Fly," and he for gets to un-key the mic. Then he tries again, and again fails to release the button. Now I know that he is at station one 150 feet from me. Out I go and tell him when you stop talking, release the button. Now the back side starts in using their own made up call signs. "Heated Horse Fly, this is Road Apple. What's your 20?" One joke transmission after another. The old watchman loses it and refuses to carry the radio.

I was out looking for the watchman when I entered the grandstand bar. I was immediately aware of a strong smell of whiskey in the bar. I looked over at the bar area and there on the bar was a large gray cat hissing and growling at me. The cat reached out a paw and hit the button on the drink dispenser. A shot of booze hit the bar. The cat lapped it up and hissed and growled again. I threw a form that was on a table at the cat. The cat ran off into the clubhouse. I informed the back side of the intruder in the bar.

They send Heated Horse Fly over to help find the cat. It was like trying to find water in a sieve. We do find the watchman, and tell him about the cat. The watchman tells me the cat has been doing this for years. He never thought it was important to let anyone know that this was a problem. I had to explain to him that every time the cat went on a bender, the bar was going to be short in the till, leaving us wasting time trying to catch a bartender skimming drinks.

In a way I was glad the watchman had witnessed the cat drinking. I wasn't sure my report would be believed by management without someone else having witnessed such an event. I secured the booze dispenser as best I could and then went in and wrote my report.

About an hour later I was re-checking the bar. When I came to the steps leading to the bar from the grandstand I hear the cat let out a scream and off the bar roof he comes, landing in a pile of trash about 10 feet ahead of me next to the track wall. The cat never moved, so I thought it was dead. It was about 50 feet from the roof to the ground. I added the incident to my report. I left a note for the cleanup crew to dispose of the cat.

About a week later the cat was back, and he was pissed off. The front office instituted tighter controls to make sure the booze dispensers were secure.

Nothing is ever as it first appears. The bar staff were not skimming drinks. The watchman was not doing his job. The cat was not dead. The back side guards were not going to pass on this opportunity to spice up their normally boring graveyard shift with weeks of levity over the antics of Heated Bar Fly.

Part Six:

Comments on liberalism and the Military

Chapter 21

Fort Lewis Shooting

In the 30 years I served as a police officer, I never fired my weapon with intent to kill a person. I came close several times. It took retirement and a job at the local military base to make that happen.

About 6 of us were working the north gate. We were alerted to a visit by the Commanding General. That meant we had to be on our toes. When he came through, security was tightened. He had just passed the gate when a truck came in, and the driver did not have the proper pass. He was sent to the screening area and the MPs were talking to him when all hell broke loose.

When stuff like what I am about to relate happens, there is a period of intense reckoning in which time is compressed and fear is magnified. The greatest fears of the various individuals are magnified. As the action is happening, the individual is reacting to the facts at hand and the fear of the unknown.

When the action is over, the individual is judged by the known facts. The fears that caused the inevitable overreaction to the stimulus are discounted. Monday morning quarterback syndrome takes over. Inevitably people are punished for actions they should be given medals for. This was the case, in my opinion, at the Fort's north gate shooting.

The facts were these. Shortly after the Commanding General had passed through the gate, a truck was stopped attempting to gain entry to the post. The driver was allegedly going to a job fair being held at the north fort E M club. The truck that he was driving was later determined to be stolen. The driver was a wanted felon.

When he was stopped, he panicked and spun the truck around at the gate and attempted to run over several guards in the process. From my view, it appeared that he had indeed run over one of the guards.

As it turned out, the truck either missed him all together or it bounced over him without the tires striking the guard. He had only minor injuries. Five guards opened fire on the truck. I fired 3 rounds myself as the truck was turning to leave. The MP on the gate emptied his weapon as the truck was coming at him. The driver of the truck had a look of determination as he charged the truck toward the guards and vehicles stopped at the gate. The whole thing was menacing and very dangerous.

The 20/20 hind sighted chief of security saw the event as rather less threatening than I. The MP was relieved of his post and sent back to his guard unit with a reprimand. When I heard, this I went to the head of security and lodged a protest. I don't know if he took my view on the matter to heart, but he got my point.

It is no wonder that policing is so difficult and breeds the attitude that we should do the minimum and reap the maximum.

Every one of these kids I worked with were war vets. They saw the threat for what it was a dangerous and unnecessary provocation by an individual bent on harm. This individual was solely responsible for the shooting and any consequences that may have resulted from discharging those weapons.

All those young men that stood in his way should have been given commendations. As it was, they were lucky not to be prosecuted for assault on the driver. If I had not been there, I believe they would have been. I was having none of it.

Training troops

Of all the military jobs I have had, I think training troops on weapons was the best. Shooting has always come easy for me. In the Army, I qualified as expert and I mastered all the weapons we used at the fort easily. I liked getting troops zeroed with their rifles. You got a chance to know them and diagnose the little problems that helped them to shoot better. As civilians, they could relax with us and learn. We didn't mess around we got down with them and laid in the same mud puddles.

With the heavy machine guns, the biggest problem some of them had was bracketing a target –they would go one click on the site adjustment when they needed to go five or ten. I was trying to get them to use two adjustments rather than five or six to zero in on a target. Shoot, over shoot the other way, and come back to center. It conserved ammo and time.

There is a line in the movie Full Metal Jacket where the drill sergeant says, "they are all the same; they are all the lowest form of life – maggots." All are equal in the eyes of the drill instructor. Then he renames them as Pvt. Joker, Pvt. Snowball, Pvt. Cowboy, and Pvt. Gomer Pyle, a new baptism as such. Then he says, "You can give your heart to God, but your ass belongs to the corps."

If you have achieved accolades, graduated at the top of your class, and enjoyed success in all things and yet have never been to boot camp, you are still the lowest form of animal life. You just don't know it yet. Ignorance is bliss.

Racism in the military vs. the racism of liberalism

My personal experience with racism in the military comes from the four years of my first enlistment starting in 1963 and from my employment by the military at a military post after 9/11/2001.

In 1963, white and colored troops in the army largely got along well on base, but did not mix to any great extent off base. This was true both in the states and overseas and the issues were not discussed. After 9/11/2001, things had changed. Race issues were openly discussed among troops and civilian employees. They classified themselves as white people, black people, brown people, yellow people. As I had been a police officer for thirty years, I classified myself as "The Blue People." This was not only because I was a police officer, but even though I am 1/8 Cherokee, I took after my Scottish heritage which is so white I tended to have a blue tint at the end of winter. In summer I tan red. The Range Team seemed to get a kick out of that.

They use the word "People" when discussing race. I was struck by this fact. It is a subtle but effective way of equalizing folks. We may be different shades but we are all people.

If the liberal KKK could have heard the good-natured banter that went on between the troops during down times at the fort, they would have gone ballistic. The Old KKK used race and religion to divide us. The New KKK liberalism uses the same tactics.

What's the difference? Hate Is Hate!

I remember one discussion over whether we would ever have a black president. The black people argued that it would never happen in their life time The brown, white, and blue people mostly said it would happen, and soon. Colin Powell was held up as a black person who had a chance of being elected. The black people said that America was far to racist to let that happen. I tried to assure them that, except for the branch of American Liberalism I call the New KKK (and even that is multi-racial now), America was eager to see a black president. Unfortunately, I was right. They elected a liberal KKK leader to office. He is doing his best to stir up hate again – not just between the races, though that is being used; they are stirring up a new kind of hate between philosophies. The tactics they use are those of liberal professor Saul Alinsky and those like him. No one knows bigotry better than a cop and the cops that know it the best are cops with a hint of color they catch bigotry from all sides.

Having lived through the changes of the 50's 60's 70's and 80's and now the new millennium, I can make this observation. The bad things in general are never as bad as they are portrayed to be by those that abdicate change. The grand expectations of the advocates of change are never turn out as grand as expected

Everyone wants that light rail but it's just not what we want to use to get to town. Everyone wants social Justus, but we are not going to work hard to get ahead and give half of what we worked for to some guy that just wants to lie around and smoke his dope. There is no social Justus there is only work hard and get what you can get. Help the poor when you can, because poor you were when you were born and poor you will be when you die.

The rise of the band of brothers Known as anarchist is an offshoot of the liberal agenda. They are all about tearing down the underpinnings of American experiment, the Christion Religion, hard work, and freedom. They hate the very peace that these values rest on.

The time has come to get over the divisions and restore civility. Let us get away from Saul Alinsky and back to binding up the nation's wounds.

As I said in the beginning, the lesson is clear:

Don't let your personal feelings about people effect your judgment about anything.

Printed in the United States
By Bookmasters